UNITED NATIONS CONFERENCE ON TRADE AND DEVELOPMENT

INVESTOR–STATE DISPUTE SETTLEMENT AND IMPACT ON INVESTMENT RULEMAKING

UNITED NATIONS
New York and Geneva, 2007

NOTE

As the focal point in the United Nations system for investment and technology, and building on 30 years of experience in those areas, UNCTAD, through DITE, promotes understanding of key issues, particularly matters related to foreign direct investment and transfer of technology. DITE also assists developing countries in attracting and benefiting from FDI and in building their productive capacities and international competitiveness. The emphasis is on an integrated policy approach to investment, technological capacity-building and enterprise development.

The term "country" as used in this study also refers, as appropriate, to territories or areas. The designations employed and the presentation of the material do not imply the expression of any opinion whatsoever on the part of the Secretariat of the United Nations concerning the legal status of any country, territory, city or area, or of its authorities, or concerning the delimitation of its frontiers or boundaries. In addition, the designations of country groups are intended solely for statistical or analytical convenience and do not necessarily express a judgment about the stage of development reached by a particular country or area in the development process.

The following symbols have been used in the tables:

Two dots (..) indicate that data are not available or are not separately reported. Rows in tables have been omitted in those cases where no data are available for any of the elements in the row.

A hyphen (-) indicates that the item is equal to zero or its value is negligible.

A blank in a table indicates that the item is not applicable.

A slash (/) between dates representing years (e.g. 1994/1995) indicates a financial year.

Use of a dash (–) between dates representing years (e.g. 1994–1995) signifies the full period involved, including the beginning and end years.

References to "dollars" ($) are to United States dollars, unless otherwise indicated.

Annual rates of growth or change, unless otherwise stated, refer to annual compound rates.

Because of rounding, details and percentages in tables do not necessarily add up to totals.

The material contained in this study may be freely quoted with appropriate acknowledgement.

UNCTAD/ITE/IIA/2007/3

UNITED NATIONS PUBLICATION
Sales No. E.07.II.D.10
ISBN 978-92-1-112720-1
ISSN 1814-2001

PREFACE

The secretariat of the United Nations Conference on Trade and Development (UNCTAD) is implementing a programme on international investment arrangements. The programme seeks to help developing countries participate as effectively as possible in international investment rulemaking. It embraces policy research and development, including the preparation of a series of issues papers; human resources capacity-building and institution-building, including national seminars, regional symposia and training courses; and support to intergovernmental consensus-building. The programme is implemented by a team led by James Zhan. Khalil Hamdani provides overall guidance to the Programme.

This paper is part of a new *Series on International Investment Policies for Development*. It builds on and expands UNCTAD's *Series on Issues in International Investment Agreements*. Like the previous one, this new series is addressed to government officials, corporate executives, representatives of non-governmental organizations, officials of international agencies and researchers.

The series seeks to provide balanced analysis of issues that may arise in the context of international approaches to investment rulemaking and their impact on development. Its purpose is to contribute to a better understanding of difficult technical issues and their interaction, and of innovative ideas that could contribute to an increase in the development dimension of international investment agreements.

The series is produced by a team led by James Zhan. The team members are Amare Bekele, Hamed El-Kady, Anna Joubin-Bret, Joachim Karl, Marie-Estelle Rey and Jörg Weber. Khalil Hamdani provides overall guidance. The members of the Review Committee are Mark Kantor, Mark Koulen, Peter Muchlinski, Antonio Parra, Patrick Robinson, Pierre Sauvé, Karl P. Sauvant, M. Sornarajah and Kenneth Vandevelde.

The present paper was prepared by Roberto Echandi on the basis of inputs from the secretariat. It served as the UNCTAD background document for the APEC Investment Facilitation Initiative: A Cooperative Effort with UNCTAD and Other Multilateral Institutions, held in Mexico on 1 and 2 October 2006. It was subsequently revised in the light of that meeting's discussions and comments received from participants. Those comments are gratefully acknowledged. Hamed El-Kady, Anna Joubin-Bret and Jörg Weber helped finalize the study. The paper was desktop published by Teresita Ventura.

The contribution of the APEC secretariat to this study is gratefully acknowledged. The Mexico meeting of the APEC Investment Facilitation Initiative was financed through the APEC TILF (Trade and Investment Liberalization and Facilitation) Fund, which was contributed by Japan.

Supachai Panitchpakdi
Secretary-General of UNCTAD

Geneva, September 2007

CONTENTS

FIGURES

ABBREVIATIONS

ASEAN	Association of Southeast Asian Nations
BIT	bilateral investment treaty
DTT	double taxation treaty
EFTA	European Free Trade Association
EIA	economic integration agreement
FTA	free trade agreement
ICJ	International Court of Justice
ICSID	International Centre for the Settlement of Investment Disputes
IIA	international investment agreement
ISDS	investor–State dispute settlement
NAFTA	North American Free Trade Agreement
UNCITRAL	United Nations Commission on International Trade Law

EXECUTIVE SUMMARY

Investment treaty provisions on investor–State dispute settlement have frequently been used in recent years, and as a result there has been in an increase in arbitral tribunal awards touching upon key procedural and substantive aspects of investment law. This has contributed to the development of a jurisprudence that, although it is still taking shape, has impacted on the evolution of investment rule-making, as witnessed in recent bilateral investment treaties and economic integration agreements with investment provisions.

Indeed, as demonstrated by this paper, the experience with the investor–State dispute settlement of a number of countries (mostly in the Asia-Pacific region) appears to have influenced the development of new international investment agreements (IIAs) by those countries. Observing how previous IIAs were interpreted and applied by arbitral tribunals, their Governments have come up with new provisions and new language, which address most of the problems that arose in the context of investment disputes. Thus, the definition of "investment" has been made more precise, several provisions dealing with standards of protection have been redrafted and clarified, the concept of transparency in the context of investment agreements has been improved and redefined, and it has been made clear that investment protection and liberalization must not be pursued at the expense of other key public policy objectives. Furthermore, investor–State dispute settlement procedures have been updated and modernized through, inter alia, fostering the provision of more information for civil society and its   increased participation in those procedures.

Although inferring trends in jurisprudence arising from investor–State dispute settlement cases has to be handled with caution, this study suggests that two important lessons can be derived from practice over the last decade. First, the increase in investment disputes has tested the wisdom of negotiating IIAs with extremely broad and imprecise provisions delegating to arbitral tribunals the task of identifying the meaning that the disputed provision should have. Second, when negotiating IIAs countries should pay attention not only to the wording of the agreement, but also to the interaction between the IIA and the arbitration convention(s) referred to in the IIA.

From a systemic perspective, it is noteworthy that most countries that are parties to the emerging *new generation* of IIAs that reflect investor–State dispute settlement experience are also still parties to numerous "old" IIAs containing provisions using the same broad and imprecise language that has triggered investment disputes elsewhere. The resultant risk of incoherence is especially high for developing countries that lack expertise and bargaining power in investment rule-making, and that may have to conduct negotiations on the basis of divergent model agreements of their negotiating partners.

However, the growing legal sophistication of investment dispute resolution also points to a further strengthening of the rule of law at the international level that should benefit developing countries that lack the political and economic power of developed nations. Furthermore, the increased number of arbitrations may also motivate developing host countries to improve domestic administrative practices and laws in order to avoid future disputes; this would further strengthen the predictability and stability of the legal framework that the conclusion of IIAs was supposed to produce in the first place.

INTRODUCTION

The settlement of disputes between investors and the countries in which they are established is a key aspect of investment protection under international investment agreements (IIAs). The majority of IIAs contain provisions on investor–State dispute settlement (ISDS). Although they had formed part of IIAs for more than 40 years, it was only in the last decade that international investors started to invoke those mechanisms to enforce the standards of treatment and protection granted by the agreements (UNCTAD 2005a; 2003).

ISDS activity during the last decade has generated a substantial number of cases touching upon key procedural and substantive aspects of investment law, thus fostering the development of a jurisprudence that, although it is still taking shape, is likely to evolve in the future. The aim of this study is to take stock of, and to analyze, the major developments in the interpretation of procedural and substantive IIA provisions as contained in bilateral investment treaties (BITs) and economic integration agreements (EIAs) with investment provisions. It will consider not only the statistical aspects of this development, but also the impact of arbitral decisions on the evolution of investment rulemaking. In particular, it will explain how ISDS experience has influenced the development of new IIAs, including the refinement of treaty provisions and the inclusion of a series of procedural and substantive innovations in those agreements.

The study contains four main sections. Section I presents an overview of the context in which investment negotiations have taken place over the last decade. Section II focuses on the major developments in ISDS jurisprudence during that period. Starting with a statistical overview of investment disputes, the analysis then examines the major issues that have arisen in the interpretation of IIAs over the last decade, covering aspects both procedural and substantive.

Inferring trends in ISDS jurisprudence requires a cautious approach. It is difficult to extract the essence of case law when the latter is based on the interpretation of IIAs, which, although apparently similar, in fact have provisions with different wording, and may thus entail very distinct legal effects. Furthermore, arbitral awards are rendered in a particular factual context that is often unique to the dispute under consideration. Thus, one has to be careful when making general statements regarding the interpretation of a particular standard of treatment or protection by arbitration tribunals. Any trend in this regard should always be placed in its appropriate context, and that is why section II endeavours to be as factual as possible.

Section III focuses on the impact of the ISDS experience on investment rulemaking. It presents the main features of a *new generation* of IIAs and explains how these respond to the challenges deriving from the interpretation of substantive and procedural provisions included in previous IIAs. Section IV addresses the implications of all those developments for countries, emphasizing the particular needs of developing countries. It also presents some conclusions and reflections on possible next steps that countries could take to implement the lessons learned from the ISDS experience.

I. TRENDS IN INTERNATIONAL INVESTMENT RULEMAKING: TREATY CONTEXT

A. Growing universe of agreements

Since the 1990s, the universe of IIAs has expanded substantially. By end 2006, the cumulative number of BITs stood at 2,573. However, the rate of increase in the annual number of BITs has been in decline since 2001, when 183 agreements were concluded. The number of double taxation treaties (DTTs) has also continued to expand. By end 2006 there were over 2,651 such treaties (figure 1).

Figure 1. Number of BITs and DTTs concluded, cumulative, 1995–2006

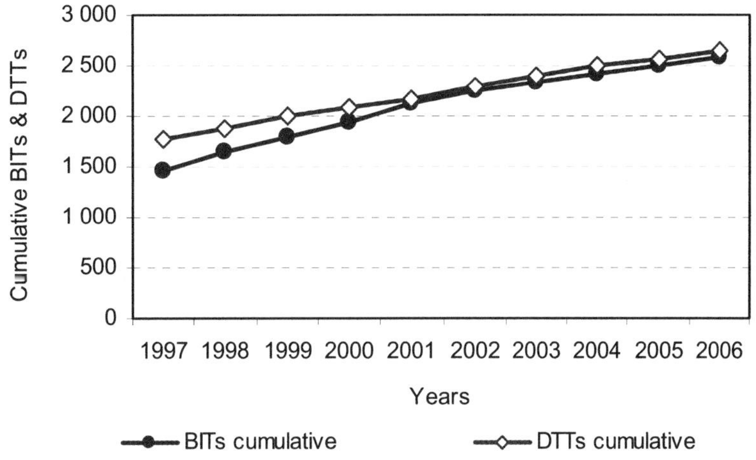

Source: UNCTAD (www.unctad.org/iia).

The universe of IIAs includes some renegotiated BITs. By end 2006, at least 110 BITs were the product of renegotiation. For instance, in 2005 China renegotiated BITs with Belgium-Luxembourg, the Czech Republic, Portugal, Slovakia and Spain, while Germany renegotiated BITs with Egypt and Yemen. The trend towards renegotiation of BITs is expected to increase further since many BITs were signed in the 1990s with an average initial duration of 10 years.

In recent years, international investment rules have also increasingly been adopted as part of bilateral, regional, interregional and plurilateral agreements that address, and seek to facilitate, trade and investment transactions. These agreements, in addition to containing a variable range of trade liberalization and promotion provisions, contain commitments to liberalize and/or to protect investment flows between the parties (UNCTAD 2006a). The number of such agreements has been growing steadily and by end 2006 exceeded 240. At least 30 new agreements were concluded between January 2005 and end 2006, involving 39 countries, and at least 67 others were under negotiation. Thus, while the rate at which new BITs are being concluded has slowed, the rate at which new EIAs with investment provisions have been concluded is increasing (figure 2).

Initially, most EIAs with investment provisions were concluded between countries in the same region. Since 1990s, however, countries located in different regions began to negotiate EIAs with investment provisions with one another, with the result that interregional EIAs with investment provisions now account for about 44 per cent of all such agreements.

The growth in the number of EIAs with investment provisions has been accompanied by important qualitative changes. For example, while such agreements were previously concluded principally among countries at similar levels of economic development, they are now negotiated with greater frequency between developed and developing countries.

Figure 2. The growth of EIAs with investment provisions, cumulative and per period, 1957–2006
(Number)

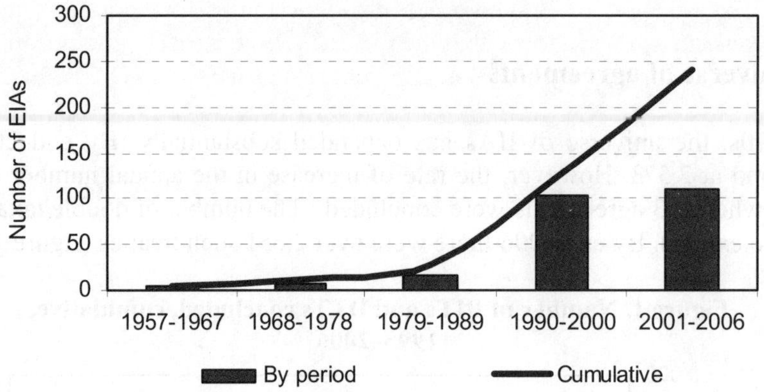

Source: UNCTAD (www.unctad.org/iia).

There is an emerging trend towards increased South–South cooperation in the conclusion of IIAs (UNCTAD 2005b). For example, between January 2005 and end 2006, 41 BITs between developing countries were signed. APEC developing members have been among the countries most active in concluding South–South BITs. For example, China, the Republic of Korea and Malaysia all have signed more than 40 BITs with other developing countries. In fact, each of those three countries has signed more agreements with other developing countries than with developed countries (UNCTAD 2006b).

The move towards greater South–South cooperation in investment matters is also evident in the conclusion of EIAs with investment provisions. By end 2006, over 90 such agreements had been signed, including 66 since 1990. Another 24 EIAs with investment provisions were being negotiated among developing countries.

B.   Expanded range of issues

Numerically, traditional BITs limited to the protection of established foreign investment continue to dominate the IIA universe. Nevertheless, a growing number of BITs contain more sophisticated investment protection provisions as well as liberalization commitments.

Also, EIAs with investment provisions show a high degree of variation in their scope and content, extending to services, intellectual property rights, competition policy, government procurement, temporary entry for business persons, transparency, the environment and labour rights. EIAs with investment provisions recently concluded by countries such as Australia, Chile, Japan, Singapore and the United States are particularly comprehensive and detailed.

Not all recent IIAs have followed this pattern, however. Some agreements have remained rather narrow in their coverage of investment issues. They are limited to establishing a framework for cooperation on promotion of foreign investments. Recent examples include the bilateral Trade and Investment Cooperation Agreements between Canada and South Africa (1998); and the ASEAN Framework Agreements with China, India and the Republic of Korea (2002, 2003 and 2005 respectively). They establish general principles with respect to further investment liberalization, promotion and protection and pave the way for the future creation of a free trade and investment area. Other examples include a number of framework agreements on trade and investment relations between the United States and countries in Africa, Asia and the Middle East. The cooperation provided for typically aims at creating favourable conditions for encouraging investment, notably through the exchange of information. It is also common for such agreements to set up consultative committees or a similar institutional arrangement between the parties to follow up on the implementation of negotiated commitments and to discuss and study possible obstacles to market access for trade and to the establishment of investment.

The more issues an IIA addresses, the more complex the agreement and the greater the likelihood of overlaps and inconsistencies with other investment-related treaties to which the country is a party. At the same time, the greater variation of IIAs presents an opportunity for adopting various approaches to promoting international investment flows that better reflect the special circumstances of countries at different levels of economic development and in different regions (UNCTAD 2006b; 2006c).

C. Increased sophistication and complexity

International investment rules are becoming increasingly sophisticated and complex. This, however, does not necessarily imply a greater degree of stringency. For example, the greater complexity may be the result of an effort to define an obligation with greater specificity and thereby to clarify its scope and application.

Some recent IIAs include significant revisions of the wording of various substantive treaty obligations. One major impetus for these revisions was the conclusion and implementation of the North American Free Trade Agreement (NAFTA) (1992) between Canada, Mexico and the United States. As will be shown below, arbitrations under the investor–State dispute resolution provision of NAFTA raised issues or resulted in arbitrations that prompted the parties to reconsider some of the language used in their IIAs. For example, the United States subsequently modified the language of its BITs and EIAs to clarify the meaning of "fair and equitable treatment" and the concept of indirect expropriation. Both changes were intended to limit the scope that arbitral tribunals might otherwise have given to the relevant provisions of the BITs (UNCTAD 2006b; 2006c).

Similarly, some recent IIAs have made significant innovations in investor–State dispute resolution procedures. An objective is to increase transparency by authorizing open hearings, publication of related documents and the submission of *amicus curiae* ("friend of the court") briefs by non-disputants who have an interest in the outcome of the dispute. Another goal of the innovations is to promote judicial economy by providing for early dismissal of frivolous claims and by attempting to prevent the presentation of the same claim in multiple forums. Other changes, intended to foster sound and consistent results, include provisions for an appeals mechanism and for consultation with the treaty parties on certain issues (ibid.).

II. TRENDS IN INTERNATIONAL INVESTMENT RULEMAKING: ARBITRATION PRACTICE

A. Developments in investor–State dispute settlement over the last decade

Provisions concerning ISDS have been included in IIAs since the 1960s. However, the use of these provisions to institute arbitral proceedings has been rare until recently. Between 1987 – when the first investor–State dispute based on a BIT was recorded in the arbitral proceedings of the World Bank's International Centre for Settlement of Investment Disputes (ICSID)[1] – and April 1998 only 14 BIT-related cases had been brought before ICSID, and only two awards and two other settlements had been issued (UNCTAD 1998, p. 140).[2]

However, since the late 1990s, the number of cases has grown enormously. The cumulative number of treaty-based cases had risen to at least 259 by the end of 2006 (figure 3), with 161 brought before ICSID (including ICSID's Additional Facility) and 92 before other arbitration forums (the exact venue for six cases was not known at the time of writing) (UNCTAD 2006d). In 2006, 29 investor-State cases were filed under IIAs. That is the lowest number of known treaty-based cases filed since the year 2000, and it suggests a considerable slowdown in the number of cases brought. However, since the ICSID arbitration facility is the only facility to maintain a public registry of claims, this could also indicate that arbitration activity has shifted into the less public domain of other arbitral venues. International investment disputes can also arise from contracts between investors and Governments; a number of such disputes are (or have been) brought before ICSID, or submitted to other institutional arbitration systems or ad hoc arbitration. They have not been included in these data, except where there is also a treaty-based claim at stake. More than two thirds (70 per cent) of the 259 known claims were filed within the past four years, with virtually none of them initiated by Governments (UNCTAD 2006d; 2005a; 2005c).[3]

These figures do not include cases where a party announced its intention to submit a claim to arbitration, but has not yet actually begun the arbitration. If these cases are ultimately submitted to arbitration, the number of pending claims will grow further. Some disputes are settled either before arbitration starts or after it has started.[4] The total number of treaty-based investment arbitrations is impossible to measure; the figures above represent only those claims that were disclosed by the parties or arbitral institutions.[5] Even where the existence of a claim has been made public, such as in the case of a claim listed in the ICSID registry, the information about such a claim is often quite minimal. Similarly, from the information in the ICSID database it is not possible to ascertain whether a claim is based on an IIA or on a State contract. Under other arbitration rules, the details of a claim and its resolution are likely to become public only if one of the disputants discloses that information. It is significant that 40 per cent of the discovered claims occur under these rules. It is therefore likely that the actual number of claims instituted under non-ICSID rules is larger than the number known.

Figure 3. Known investment treaty arbitrations, cumulative and newly instituted cases, 1987-2006

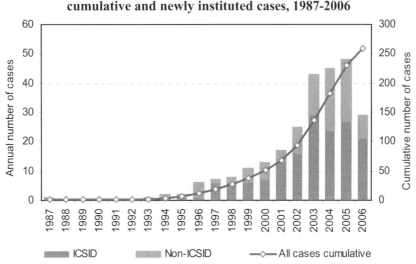

Source: UNCTAD.

The surge in the number of claims can be attributed to several factors. First, increases in international investment flows are likely to lead to more occasions for disputes, and more occasions for disputes combined with more IIAs are likely to lead to more cases.[6] Second, with larger numbers of IIAs in place, more investor–State disputes are likely to involve an alleged violation of a treaty provision and more of them are likely to be within the ambit of agreed dispute settlement procedures. Another reason may be the greater complexity of recent IIAs, and the regulatory difficulties in implementing them properly. Furthermore, as news of large, successful claims spreads, more investors may be encouraged to utilize the investor–State dispute resolution mechanism. Greater transparency in arbitration (e.g. within NAFTA) may also be a factor in giving greater visibility to this legal avenue for dispute settlement.

At least 70 Governments – 44 of them in the developing world, 14 in developed countries and 12 in South-East Europe and the Commonwealth of Independent States – have been involved in investment treaty arbitration. Argentina tops the list with 42 claims lodged against it (39 of these disputes relate at least in part to that country's financial crisis). (No new arbitration cases were brought against Argentina in the first 11 months of 2006, and only one notice of intent was registered at ICSID in that period.) Mexico continues to have the second highest number of known claims (17). The United States and the Czech Republic have the third highest number of claims filed against them, with 11 each. The Russian Federation (9 claims), Moldova (9), India (9), Egypt (8), Ecuador (8), Romania (7), Poland (7), Canada (7) and Ukraine (6) also figure prominently.

In several instances, a multitude of claims have been lodged in relation to a single investment or against a particular government action. In the Argentine cases, a series of emergency measures and policies have occasioned lawsuits brought by several dozen companies. In the case of India, the disputed Dabhol Power project led to at least two BIT claims by the project companies, as well as seven BIT claims by the project lenders. All of these claims against India have since been settled. At other times, a single arbitration procedure may have several dozens of individual claimants, as is the case in NAFTA arbitration between individual investors in tourist real estate and Mexico, and in the case of NAFTA arbitration against the United States initiated by more than 100 individual claimants in the beef industry.[7]

The vast majority of claims have been brought under BITs, several of the cases involving also contractual disputes between the State and the investor. Arbitration cases have dealt with the whole range of investment activities and all kinds of investments, including privatization contracts and State concessions. Measures that have been challenged include emergency laws put in place during a financial crisis, value-added taxes, rezoning of land from agricultural use to commercial use, measures on hazardous waste facilities, issues related to the intent to divest shareholdings of public enterprises to a foreign investor, and treatment at the hands of media regulators. Disputes have involved provisions such as those on fair and equitable treatment, non-discrimination, expropriation, and the scope and definition of agreements.

The increase in the number of investment disputes has had two significant effects. First, these disputes are resulting in awards that interpret the legal obligations of the contracting parties. This in turn has caused some countries to re-examine and reconsider the scope and extent of such obligations. Indeed, as will be shown below, the ISDS experience over the last decade appears to have a significant impact on investment rule-making, leading some countries to develop a new generation of IIAs with distinct normative features.

Second, the increase in the number of investment disputes poses a particular challenge for developing countries. Their financial implications can be substantial, from the point of view of the costs of the arbitration proceedings and the awards rendered. Information about the level of damages being sought by investors tends to be patchy and unreliable. Even ascertaining the amounts sought by foreign investors can be difficult, as most cases are still at a preliminary stage and, under the ICSID system; claimants are not obliged to quantify their claims until after the jurisdictional stage has been completed. Claims proceeding under other rules of arbitration are also difficult to quantify. It is, nonetheless, clear that some claims involve large sums (UNCTAD 2006d; 2005a). Furthermore, even defending against claims that are not ultimately successful costs money.

B.   Interpretation of IIAs: Dispute settlement procedural issues

One of the main effects of the dramatic increase in the number of treaty-based investor–State disputes over the last decade has been to generate a growing body of jurisprudence in international investment law. Numerous investor–State arbitration tribunals have interpreted provisions of IIAs dealing with key substantive standards of protection and treatment for foreign investors and their investments. Arbitration tribunals have also dealt with issues related to the procedural aspects of ISDS mechanisms included in most IIAs. This section presents an overview of the evolving case law with respect to key procedural matters related to ISDS. (The next section will focus on the jurisprudence related to substantial issues that is still taking shape.)

From the outset, the reader should be aware of two important caveats. First, any analysis attempting to identify trends in the evolution of jurisprudence related to IIAs has to be extremely cautious. Any questions in this context neither could nor should be answered in the abstract as the wording of each IIA is unique and must be construed according to its own terms. In that regard, this paper attempts only to illustrate some salient findings concerning specific cases and to evidence the implications of using particular models of treaty language.

Second, the jurisprudence on the procedural aspects of ISDS is often based on the interpretation of not only the ISDS provisions of the applicable IIA, but also the specific wording of other international arbitration conventions. Traditionally, ISDS provisions in numerous IIAs have tended to be general and laconic – in particular, in the case of the traditional model of BITs – and have often been limited to specifying the different arbitration venues available to the investor for the adjudication of the dispute. Thus, numerous procedural aspects of the arbitration process are often not regulated in the texts of the IIAs themselves. Instead, many treaties have frequently tended to rely on existing arbitration rules to clarify these matters, principally the ICSID Convention and/or the Arbitration Rules of the United Nations Commission on International Trade Law (UNCITRAL).[8] As the majority of the treaty-based investor–State disputes have been submitted to ICSID, it is not surprising that a significant part of the jurisprudence related to ISDS procedural aspects in fact deals with the interpretation of the ICSID Convention and its interaction with the applicable IIA.

Most of the procedural issues addressed in recent disputes have tended to concentrate on questions related to the jurisdiction of the arbitral tribunals to hear a particular case. However, arbitral tribunals have also dealt with other procedural matters related to the conduct of the investor–State dispute settlement proceedings. Each of those two categories of procedural matters will be dealt with below.

1.   Matters related to jurisdiction

a.   The definition of investor: Indirect claims/ownership and control

IIAs apply to investments made by investors of one contracting party in the territory of the other contracting party. Thus, in determining the scope of application of the IIAs, and consequently, the jurisdiction of arbitral tribunals, a key aspect relates to the definition of the *investor* entitled to use the *investor*–State dispute settlement procedures. Over the last decade, arbitral tribunals have dealt with various issues related to this question, and have interpreted treaty provisions in a way that has led to awards with significant implications. On this particular subject, recent ISDS jurisprudence has tended to concentrate on two broad categories. First, in order to determine whether they have jurisdiction *ratione personae*, arbitral tribunals have addressed the question of the relevant criteria for determining the nationality of a natural and/or legal person. The second category relates to the rights that minority shareholders, non-controlling and indirect shareholders may have under ISDS provisions of the IIAs.

(i) Jurisdiction ratione personae: Determination of nationality of natural persons

One of the issues addressed by various arbitration tribunals has been the kind of link that a particular investor – either a natural or a legal person – should have with the countries that are parties to the applicable IIA in order to justify the protection under the agreement.

With respect to natural persons, most IIAs have traditionally protected investors who have the nationality of one contracting party in the territory of the other contracting party. Thus, the typical definition of a national of a party used in most treaties is a natural person recognized by that party's domestic law as a national or a citizen. However, the experience in the application of IIAs over the last decade has shown that the determination of whether a particular natural person is a covered investor, and thus entitled to use the ISDS provisions under the applicable treaty, is often not a straightforward matter.

The relevance of this question has been particularly important for cases submitted to ICSID, as Article 25 (1) of the ICSID Convention explicitly provides, inter alia, that the "[…] *jurisdiction of the Centre shall extend only to those legal disputes arising directly out of an investment, between a Contracting State […] and a national of **another** Contracting State […]*" (emphasis added). This means that the investor's status under ICSID proceedings is subject to a positive and a negative nationality requirement. The investor not only has to be a national of a contracting state, but also must not be a national of the host country contracting party. Furthermore, Article 25 (2) (a) of the ICSID Convention provides that this nationality requirement must be met at two different moments: first, on the date on which the parties consented to submit the dispute to arbitration, and, second, on the date on which the request for arbitration is registered at the Centre by the Secretary-General.

The parameter repeatedly used by arbitration tribunals to determine whether a person is a national of a particular country has tended to be the law of the country whose nationality is claimed. For instance, in *Champion Trading v. Egypt* [9] the tribunal was faced with the question of determining whether the non-corporate complainants – three individuals who had been born in the United States, but who were the sons of a father born in Egypt – complied with the requirement in Article 25 (2) (a) of the ICSID Convention. That provision reads as follows:

> "*(2) "National of another Contracting State" means:*
> *(a) any natural person who had the nationality of a Contracting State other than the State party to the dispute on the date on which the parties consented to submit such dispute to conciliation or arbitration as well as on the date on which the request was registered pursuant to paragraph (3) of Article 28 or paragraph (3) of Article 36, **but does not include any person who on either date also had the nationality of the Contracting State party to the dispute** […].*" (emphasis added)

Under Egyptian law, a child born of an Egyptian father, either in or outside Egypt, automatically acquires Egyptian nationality at birth. Although the father of the claimants had become a citizen of the United States, the Egyptian Government, which acted as defendant in this case, argued that the father had also remained an Egyptian national, as he had never given up his Egyptian nationality and, therefore, his three sons had automatically acquired Egyptian nationality. Thus, Egypt argued that the claimants had dual nationality, one of them being the Egyptian one, and thus could not be considered "nationals of another Contracting State" for the purposes of Article 25 (2) (a) of the ICSID Convention.

The claimants argued that the Egyptian nationality of the three individual claimants did not correspond to the prevailing definition of nationality in international law. They argued that if they were to be considered Egyptian it was only because Egyptian law conferred Egyptian nationality on them at birth. The claimants further submitted that, in fact, they had never had any particular ties or relations with Egypt, and thus, such an involuntary nationality should not be taken into account when interpreting the ICSID Convention. Making reference to *Nottebohm*[10] and to the Iran–United States Claims Tribunal, Case N°

A/18,[11] the claimants also submitted that under international law the nationality of a person should be determined on the basis of the existence of a genuine link with the country of asserted nationality.

Pointing to the undisputed fact that the claimants had conducted transactions related to the investment in question by referring to their Egyptian nationality, the arbitral tribunal found that the investors had dual nationality, and thus, that it lacked jurisdiction over the claims. The tribunal considered that neither the *Nottebohm* nor the *A/18* decisions were applicable to the case, as the ICSID Convention, in Article 25(2)(a), contains a clear and specific rule regarding dual nationals. Interpreting that provision in accordance with Article 31 of the Vienna Convention on the Law of Treaties, the tribunal found that within the ordinary meaning of Article 25(2)(a) of the ICSID Convention dual nationals are excluded from invoking the protection of the Convention against the host country of the investment of which they are also citizens.[12]

The practice of referring to the national law of the country whose nationality is being claimed in order to determine whether a particular investor is a national of that country is also illustrated by *Soufraki v. United Arab Emirates*.[13] In that case, the claimant, an investor born in Italy who later became a citizen of Canada, sought the protection of the BIT between Italy and the United Arab Emirates (1995). Under Italian law, Italian citizens acquiring another nationality and residing abroad automatically lose their Italian nationality. However, Italian legislation also allows former citizens to automatically reacquire Italian nationality by taking up residence in Italy for a period of no less than one year. Within that context, the tribunal was faced with the issue of whether the claimant, by his acquisition of Canadian nationality and his taking up residence in Canada, had lost his Italian nationality, and – if that was the case – whether he had complied with the requirements set by Italian law for recovering it. Regarding which parameters to apply in order to determine the nationality of the claimant, the tribunal stated as follows:

> "55. It is accepted in international law that nationality is within the domestic jurisdiction of the State, which settles, by its own legislation, the rules relating to the acquisition (and loss) of its nationality. Article 1(3) of the BIT [between Italy and the UAE] reflects this rule. But it is no less accepted that when, in international arbitral or judicial proceedings, the nationality of a person is challenged, the international tribunal is competent to pass [judgement] upon that challenge. It will accord great weight to the nationality law of the State in question and to the interpretation and application of that law by its authorities. But it will in the end decide for itself, whether, on the facts and law before it, the person whose nationality is at issue was or was not a national of the State in question and when, and what follows from that finding. Where, as in the instant case, the jurisdiction of an international tribunal turns on an issue of nationality, the international tribunal is empowered, indeed bound, to decide that issue."[14]

In this particular case, the tribunal based its decision on the provisions of the applicable Italian legislation, and found that under Italian law the claimant had effectively lost his Italian nationality, and had not effectively demonstrated that he had complied with the residence requirements for regaining Italian nationality. Thus, the tribunal found that the claimant was not an Italian national under the laws of Italy at the two relevant times required by the ICSID Convention, namely the date of the parties´ consent to ICSID arbitration and the date on which the request for arbitration was registered with ICSID.

The trends in recent ISDS jurisprudence concerning the determination of jurisdiction *ratione personae* with regard to natural persons have important implications, which should be considered by government officials when negotiating IIAs. First, when drafting the wording of ISDS provisions in IIAs, negotiators should bear in mind that the jurisdiction *ratione personae* of arbitral tribunals, in particular those under ICSID, will be determined not only by the relevant provisions of the IIAs, but also according to the objective criteria established by Article 25 of the ICSID Convention.

Second, in principle, the question of whether a particular person is a covered national under an IIA will be determined in accordance with the domestic legislation of the country whose nationality is claimed. However, tribunals have recognized the importance of the existence of an effective link between the investor and that country.

Third, there may be potential conflicts between certain IIAs and the ICSID Convention. First, some BITs leave open the possibility for a natural person possessing the nationality of both BIT parties under their respective laws to claim treaty protection. In those cases, some of these BITs provide that a person who is a dual citizen shall be deemed to be exclusively a citizen of the State of his or her dominant and effective citizenship.[15] In this regard, it should be noted that under Article 25 of the ICSID Convention that kind of investor would not be able to submit a claim under ICSID, even if, in principle, the applicable IIA envisaged that possibility. Such investors would have to submit their claims in any other arbitration forum – if any – envisaged in the ISDS provisions of the treaty.

A second potential conflict between ISDS provisions in certain IIAs and the ICSID Convention may arise because some IIAs contain a definition of "investor" that includes not only citizens but also individuals who qualify as permanent residents under domestic law.[16] Although Article 25(2)(a) of the ICSID Convention does not require the claimant to have the nationality of the particular contracting party of the IIA the protection of which is being invoked, it requires the investor to be a national of a Contracting State of the Convention. Thus, a permanent resident of a given country, despite being a covered investor under an IIA, may yet be prevented from submitting a claim under the ICSID Convention if his/her country of effective citizenship is not a Contracting State of that Convention. In such a situation, the investor would have to resort to other arbitral forums or rules.

(ii) Jurisdiction ratione personae: Determination of nationality of legal entities

As in the case of natural persons, one of the issues frequently addressed by various ISDS arbitration tribunals has been the kind of link that a particular legal entity needs to have with the countries that are parties to the applicable IIA in order to consider such entity as a covered investor under the agreement.

With respect to juridical persons, three different criteria – in different combinations – have been traditionally used in IIAs to define their nationality. These are the place of incorporation, the location of the company's seat – also referred to as the "*siège social*", "real seat" or "principal place of business" – and the nationality of ownership or control.

The ICSID Convention does not specify any particular criteria for ascribing the nationality of a legal entity for the purposes of determining the jurisdiction *ratione personae* of arbitral tribunals. In that regard, Article 25 (2)(b) of the Convention states only as follows:

> "*(2) "National of another Contracting State" means:*
> *[…]*
> *(b) any juridical person which had the nationality of a Contracting State other than the State party to the dispute on the date on which the parties consented to submit such dispute to conciliation or arbitration and any juridical person which had the nationality of the Contracting State party to the dispute on that date and which, because of foreign control, the parties have agreed should be treated as a national of another Contracting State for the purposes of this Convention.*"

This article thus envisages two different situations under which ICSID tribunals may have jurisdiction *ratione personae* when the claimant is a juridical person. One establishes the general principle according to which the legal entity must have the nationality of a contracting State different from the host country on the date on which arbitration was consented to. The other situation addresses the case where the legal entity, despite having the nationality of the host country, is nevertheless treated as foreign as a result of being controlled by foreigners.

As regards the general principle, ICSID tribunals have traditionally tended to apply the criterion of incorporation or seat rather than control when determining the nationality of a juridical person.[17] This trend is illustrated by numerous ICSID cases, such as *Southern Pacific Properties v. Egypt*, where the claimants were considered to be from Hong Kong (China) (because they were Hong Kong corporations domiciled in Hong Kong (China)),[18] and *Kaiser Bauxite v. Jamaica*, where the claimant was found to be from the United States because "Kaiser Bauxite" was a private corporation organized under the laws of the State of Nevada.[19] An interesting case is *Tokios Tokeles v. Ukraine*, a dispute brought under the Lithuania–Ukraine BIT in which the claimant was a corporate national of Lithuania, although 99 per cent of the shareholders were nationals of Ukraine. In that case, the majority of the members of the arbitral tribunal considered that under the terms of the BIT and the ICSID Convention the nationality of the country of incorporation of the investor – and not the nationality of the controlling shareholders – was decisive for the standing of the claimant.[20]

ICSID tribunals, however, have also granted a significant degree of deference to the criteria agreed by the parties in order to determine the nationality of legal entities, insofar as those criteria are reasonable. This approach was applied in *Autopista Concesionada de Venezuela v. Venezuela*,[21] where the tribunal determined, on the basis of the terms agreed by the parties to the dispute, that the nationality of the corporate claimant – an enterprise incorporated in Florida but controlled by Mexican investors – was American.[22]

The second scenario addressed by Article 25(2)(b) of the ICSID Convention is one in which the parties to the dispute agree to consider a legal entity constituted or having its seat in the host country as a foreign investor because of foreign control. This clause therefore establishes two requirements: first, that there is an agreement between the parties to the dispute to treat a legal entity of the host country as foreign; and second, that such entity is effectively controlled by foreigners.

Regarding the first requirement, a number of IIAs explicitly provide that companies constituted in the host country but controlled by nationals of another contracting party shall be treated as nationals of the latter.[23] Other IIAs give standing not to the company established in the host country, but to the controlling investor on behalf of the company.[24] A different situation arises when the IIA does not contain any provision similar to the ones referred to above. In such a scenario, determination of whether an ICSID tribunal has jurisdiction *ratione personae* when the claimant is a legal person of the host country but controlled by foreign nationals would have to be made on a case-by-case basis. According to various ICISD tribunals, the test would be met if the specific circumstances of the case clearly indicate that this was the intention of the parties. For instance, several tribunals, such as in *Liberian Eastern Timber Corporation (LETCO) v. Liberia*[25] and *Klöckner Industrie-Anlagen GmbH and others v. Cameroon*,[26] have considered that the mere existence of an ICSID clause in a contract with a local company constitutes an agreement to treat that legal entity as a national of another Contracting State. In *Amco Asia Corporation and others v. Indonesia*,[27] the tribunal found that the ICSID Convention does not require a formal agreement to treat a local company as foreign because of foreign control. The tribunal stated:

> "*14...(ii) Nothing in the Convention, and in particular in Article 25, provides for a formal requisite of an express clause stating that the parties have decided to treat a company having legally the nationality of the Contracting State, which is a party to the dispute, as a foreign company of another Contracting State, because of the control to which it is submitted. What is needed, for the final provision of Article 25(2)(b) to be applicable, is (1) that the juridical person, party to the dispute, be legally a national of the Contracting State which is the other party and (2) that this juridical person being under foreign control, to the knowledge of the Contracting State, the parties agree to treat it as a foreign juridical person.*"[28]

Although ICSID jurisprudence has recognized the possibility of inferring the existence of an agreement to treat a local company as foreign because of foreign control on the basis of specific circumstances, ICSID tribunals have been more stringent regarding the factual determination of the existence of foreign control over the local company in order to deem the latter to be foreign.

Determining actual control over legal entities is not a simple matter. ICSID tribunals have developed an increasing awareness of the need to take a differentiated approach when dealing with this question. Various tribunals have asked whether foreigners own a majority of the shares of the enterprise concerned.[29] This parameter has been used in cases such as *Klöckner v. Cameroon*, where the tribunal found that the local company SOCAME was under the majority control of foreign interests because Klöckner and its European partners had subscribed to 51 per cent of SOCAME's capital.[30] In *LETCO v. Liberia*, French investors owned 100 per cent of the company's shares, although it had been incorporated in Liberia.[31] The missing foreign control was the decisive element in *Vacuum Salt v. Ghana* for the tribunal to determine its lack of jurisdiction. In that case, the tribunal found that only 20 per cent of the shares of the company incorporated in Ghana were in foreign hands, while nationals of Ghana owned 80 per cent.[32]

Vacuum Salt v. Ghana illustrates that for an ICSID tribunal to have jurisdiction *ratione personae*, the corporate claimant established in the host country cannot be deemed to be a foreign investor unless it is effectively controlled by nationals of another ICSID Contracting State. Thus, ICSID tribunals would not have jurisdiction if the company is controlled by foreigners who are not nationals of an ICSID Contracting State, or who are nationals of the host country of an investment. However, this rule has two important caveats.

First, ICSID jurisprudence has accepted that the effective foreign control required by Article 25(2)(b) may be not only direct but also indirect. In *Société Ouest Africaine des Bétons Industriels (SOABI) v. Senegal,* all the shares of the local company, SOABI, were owned by a company incorporated in Panama, a country that at the time was not an ICSID Contracting State. The tribunal nevertheless found that another company, Flexa, which in turn was controlled by nationals of Belgium, controlled the Panamanian enterprise. As Belgium was an ICSID Contracting State, the tribunal found that SOABI was under the indirect control of nationals of a Contracting State.[33]

Second, ICSID jurisprudence has accepted that as long as the nationals controlling the local company are nationals of another ICSID Contracting State, the requirements of Article 25(2)(b) may be fulfilled, even if the nationals concerned have dual nationality, one of the nationalities being that of the host country. In *Champion Trading v. Egypt,* one of the corporate claimants, Champion Trading Co., was incorporated in the State of Delaware. However, practically all of its capital was owned by natural persons who were nationals of the United States and Egypt. In this case, the tribunal stated:

> "*Neither the Treaty nor the Convention contain any exclusion of dual nationals as shareholders of companies of the other Contracting State, contrary to the specific exclusion of Article 25(2)(a) of the Convention regarding natural persons.*
> *The Respondents did not adduce any precedents or learned writings according to which dual nationals could not be shareholders in companies bringing an ICSID action under the Treaty. The Tribunal therefore holds that it does have jurisdiction over the claims of the two corporate Claimants.*"[34]

Another issue that arose in the context of the determination of the claimant's nationality and delimitation of the jurisdiction *ratione personae* of ISDS arbitral tribunals is related to the particular time at which the claimant must have a nationality different from that of the respondent State. This issue was contested in the NAFTA case *Loewen Group Inc. and Raymond Loewen v. United States*.[35] In particular, the focus of the controversy was on whether under NAFTA's Chapter 11 and the ICSID Additional Facility Rules, a claimant must observe a "continuous nationality rule", under which during the entire arbitration process the claimant must hold a nationality different from that of the host country.

In *Loewen v. United States* the dispute involved two claimants – one corporate, one individual – who alleged injuries to two corporations, a Canadian corporation and its American subsidiary. Unable to submit a claim under the ICSID Convention – because Canada is not a Contracting State of ICSID – Raymond Loewen, the individual investor, submitted a claim under ICSID's Additional Facility Rules and NAFTA Article 1117. Loewen submitted his claim as an "investor of a Party" entitled, by control or ownership, to bring an action on behalf of the Canadian entity. That entity in turn brought a claim on its own behalf and on behalf of its American subsidiary. After the claim had been filed, the Canadian entity was reorganized, emerging as an American company. According to the tribunal, that left no Canadian entity capable of pursuing the claim. Furthermore, the tribunal rejected Raymond Loewen's claims on the ground that he had not proved that he still had a controlling interest in his company.

The outcome in *Loewen v. United States* might have been quite different if it could have been brought under the ICSID Convention. It is generally accepted that continuous nationality is not a general requirement under Article 25 of this Convention, as it only applies at the date of consent.[36] Furthermore, it is not clear whether the ICSID Additional Facility Rules allow for a continuous nationality rule. Thus, the tribunal's decision in *Loewen v. United States* has been the subject of controversy, and it has been argued that:

> "*The assertion that there is a customary international law requiring continuous nationality up to the time of the award or judgment is in fact unsupported by sufficient authority, and there is authority, as well as arguments of principle, against it.*"[37]

In conclusion, as stated above with regard to natural persons, the ISDS jurisprudence concerning the determination of jurisdiction *ratione personae* in respect of juridical persons has significant consequences for IIA negotiations. Negotiators should take into account that the jurisdiction *ratione personae* of arbitral tribunals, in particular those under ICSID, will be determined not only by the relevant provisions of the IIAs, but also according to the objective criteria established by Article 25 of the ICSID Convention.

Second, whether a particular legal entity is a covered investor under an IIA will be determined, in general, in accordance with the criteria explicitly agreed in the treaty. Thus, if the contracting parties to an IIA purport to treat local companies of the host country as foreign investors because of foreign control, it is advisable to explicitly provide for such a possibility in the text of the agreement.

Third, there may be potential conflicts between the text of certain IIAs and the ICSID Convention. Although the latter does not define the concept of juridical persons, its wording suggests that legal personality is a requirement for the application of Article 25(2)(b). However, some IIAs include associations without legal personality in their definitions of "companies". This could leave those associations without any *jus standi* before ICSID, given that for the purposes of the Convention the precondition of legal personality is inherent in the concept of "juridical person" and is part of the objective requirements for arbitral tribunals to have jurisdiction *ratione personae*.

(iii) Minority, non-controlling and indirect shareholders

One of the issues attracting significant attention in ISDS jurisprudence on jurisdiction over the last decade has been whether minority, non-controlling or indirect shareholders have *jus standi* before ISDS arbitral tribunals. This has been the subject of much discussion, particularly – though not exclusively – in the context of the numerous cases submitted to ICSID arbitration against Argentina.

The debate stems from the fact that in the 1970s, according to traditional views of customary international law, individual shareholders did not have any mechanism to seek redress if damage was done to the company in which they had shares. The landmark case cited in this regard is *Barcelona Traction*.[38] This involved a Canadian company incorporated in Toronto, Canada, that conducted most of its operations through subsidiaries in Spain, and which was owned by majority shareholders who were nationals and residents of Belgium. After the Barcelona Traction Company was severely affected by a series of measures taken by the Government of Spain, Belgium submitted a claim to the International Court of Justice (ICJ). The main question before the ICJ was whether Belgium had the right to exercise diplomatic protection for Belgian shareholders of a Canadian company, and thus have standing before the Court.

In the *Barcelona Traction* case, the ICJ decided that the Spanish Government's actions had been taken against the company, and not against the shareholders themselves, and that the mere fact that both the company and its shareholders might suffer damage did not imply that both were entitled to claim compensation. Although the ICJ recognized that bilateral investment treaties and other instruments did provide for protection of shareholders, the Court identified those agreements as *lex specialis;* this led it to conclude that under customary international law such a rule had not yet been developed.

Most of the disputes addressing the issue of shareholders' *jus standi* over the last decade have involved contracts between the Government of the host country and companies. Although the companies were locally incorporated, their shares were directly or indirectly owned by foreign investors submitting the claims. While in some cases, foreign investors held the majority of the capital stock, they had only a minority, non-controlling interest in others. In all of these disputes, the claimants sought protection under an applicable BIT, and in most cases the disputes were submitted to ICSID arbitration tribunals. In most of the disputes involving Argentina, the respondent – often referring to the *Barcelona Traction* case – challenged the jurisdiction of the tribunals on the ground that shareholders were not entitled to submit a claim separately from the entity directly owning the investment. For instance, in both *LG&E v. Argentina*[39] and *CMS Gas Transmission Company v. Argentina*[40] the claimants were indirect investors in the sense that they were minority shareholders in the local Argentine companies holding gas distribution licences. Furthermore, both *Siemens v. Argentina*[41] and *Azurix Corp. v. Argentina*[42] involved shareholdings through indirectly owned and controlled subsidiaries.

In all of these disputes, ISDS arbitral tribunals have been consistent in providing minority, non-controlling and indirect shareholders with *jus standi* under the ICSID Convention and the applicable IIA. These decisions relied mainly on three points, which are clearly illustrated by the tribunal's findings in *CMS v. Argentina*. In that case, the tribunal first distinguished between a situation of diplomatic protection and a situation in which the investor directly seeks redress for the damage suffered. Stressing the fact that *Barcelona Traction* was a case related to diplomatic protection, the tribunal stated that it was not applicable to the factual situation of the dispute:

> "*Diplomatic protection itself has been dwindling in current international law, as the State of nationality is no longer considered to be protecting its own interest in the claim but that of the individual affected. To some extent, diplomatic protection is intervening as a residual mechanism to be resorted to in the absence of other arrangements recognizing the direct right of action by individuals. It is precisely this kind of arrangement that has come to prevail under international law, particularly in respect of foreign investments, the paramount example being that of the 1965 Convention.*"[43]

In *CMS v. Argentina*, the tribunal not only drew a distinction between diplomatic protection and individual investors' direct right of action, but also suggested that because of the worldwide expansion of IIAs a new rule might have developed under customary international law:

> "*The Tribunal therefore finds no bar in current international law to the concept of allowing claims by shareholders independently from those of the corporation concerned, not even if those shareholders are minority or non-controlling shareholders. Although it is true, as argued by the Republic of Argentina, that this is mostly the result of* lex specialis *and specific treaty arrangements that have so allowed, the fact is that* lex specialis *in this respect is so prevalent that it can now be considered the general rule, certainly in respect of foreign investments and increasingly in respect of other matters. To the extent that customary international law or generally the traditional law of international claims might have followed a different approach – a proposition that is open to debate – then that approach can be considered the exception.*"[44]

The second point made clear by the *CMS* tribunal in favour of providing *jus standi* to minority, non-controlling and indirect shareholders is based on the text of the ICSID Convention. As it does not define the term "investment", it cannot be concluded, in the tribunal's view, that the only investments covered by the Convention are those owned by majority or controlling shareholders:

"Precisely because the Convention does not define "investment", it does not purport to define the requirements that an investment should meet to qualify for ICSID jurisdiction. There is indeed no requirement that an investment, in order to qualify, must necessarily be made by shareholders controlling a company or owning the majority of its shares. It is well known incidentally that, depending on how shares are distributed, controlling shareholders can in fact own less than the majority of shares. The reference that Article 25(2)(b) makes to foreign control in terms of treating a company of the nationality of the Contracting State party as a national of another Contracting State is precisely meant to facilitate agreement between the parties, so as not to have the corporate personality interfering with the protection of the real interests associated with the investment. The same result can be achieved by means of the provisions of the BIT, where the consent may include non-controlling or minority shareholders."[45]

The third point, which completes the reasoning of the tribunal in *CMS* in favour of providing *jus standi* to indirect, minority and non-controlling shareholders, is the text of the applicable IIA. In the case in question, Article I(1)(a) of the BIT between Argentina and the United States (1992) explicitly states that "investment" comprises "*every kind of investment in the territory of one Party owned or controlled, directly or indirectly by nationals or companies of the other Party* [...]". Furthermore, this definition explicitly provides that investment includes "*a company or shares of stock or other interests in a company or interests in the assets thereof* [...]". Thus, quoting the tribunal's decision in *Lanco International Inc. v. Argentina*,[46] which had interpreted the same definition of "investment" of the Argentina–United States BIT, the *CMS* tribunal concluded that indirect, minority and non-controlling investors were covered investors under that agreement, and thus had *jus standi* before the arbitral tribunal:

"The Tribunal finds that the definition of this term in the ARGENTINA-U.S. Treaty is very broad and allows for many meanings. For example, as regards shareholder equity, the ARGENTINA-U.S. Treaty says nothing indicating that the investor in the capital stock has to have control over the administration of the company, or a majority share; thus the fact that LANCO holds an equity share of 18.3% in the capital stock of the Grantee allows one to conclude that it is an investor in the meaning of Article 1 of the ARGENTINA-U.S. Treaty. [...]"[47]

The *CMS* case, like the various other disputes addressing the issue of indirect, minority and non-controlling shareholders' *jus standi,* illustrates the implication of using a broad definition of "investor" in IIAs. As most IIAs regard shareholdings or participation in a company as a form of investment, it follows that minority, indirect and non-controlling shareholders are entitled to claims in respect of their investments. In these situations, investors have standing not because they control the enterprise, but because their shares constitute the investment. According to this logic, the relative participation of a minority shareholder in the total capital stock of the company concerned is not relevant for determining jurisdiction.[48] In this regard, there is no known case so far that sets a lower limit on the value of a shareholding that would allow the investor–State dispute settlement procedures to be used, where such a requirement is not set out in the text of the treaty itself. Thus, this latter aspect is a point to which government officials should pay attention when negotiating IIAs.

b. *Jurisdiction ratione personae: State and State entities*

In addition to the variables explained above, a determination as to whether an arbitral tribunal has jurisdiction *ratione personae* under an ISDS procedure depends on whether the dispute involves a State or an entity of the State. Indeed, investment agreements regulate the behaviour of *States* vis-à-vis foreign investors. Furthermore, the disputes submitted under the ICSID Convention explicitly require that a *State* be involved in the dispute. Article 25(1) of the ICSID Convention provides that:

"*The jurisdiction of the Centre shall extend to any legal dispute [...] between a Contracting State (or any constituent subdivision or agency of a Contracting State designated to the Centre by that State) and a national of another Contracting State [...].*"

In practice, however, foreign investors usually do not deal with the State itself. Most often, investors interact with government agencies, government-owned companies, State enterprises or administrative and judicial courts. Within this context, ISDS jurisprudence has dealt with the issue of whether, and under what circumstances, the conduct of the latter entities can be attributed to the host *State* and thus become the basis for a claim under an IIA.

To determine whether the conduct of a legal entity that is distinct from the host *State* can nevertheless be attributed to the latter, ISDS arbitration tribunals have taken into account, on the one hand, the structure of the entity concerned, comprising aspects such as its legal personality, ownership and control, and, on the other hand, the character, purposes and objectives of the functions performed by the entity whose actions are under scrutiny. Thus, arbitral tribunals have developed what became known as the "structural" and "functional" tests to determine whether actions of an entity other than the Government itself may nevertheless be attributable to the *State*, and thus generate *State* responsibility under an IIA. One of the cases in which these tests were applied in greater detail was *Emilio Agustín Maffezini v. Spain*.[49]

The dispute in this case involved the claims of an Argentine investor and his dealings with Sociedad para el Desarrollo Industrial de Galicia (SODIGA), an entity owned by the regional government of Galicia and established to promote economic development in that region of Spain. On the particular issue involved, the question before the arbitral tribunal was whether the acts complained of by the claimant, which were undertaken by SODIGA, were in fact attributable to Spain. The tribunal applied what it referred to as a "structural" and "functional" test.

Under the "structural test", the arbitrators considered whether SODIGA was a "State entity" or "State organ". For that purpose, the arbitral tribunal conducted an assessment of the company's legal personality and examined whether SODIGA was established by law as a government entity. The tribunal noted that SODIGA was not defined as an administrative agency by Spanish public law, but was constituted under private law as a commercial company. It thus concluded that SODIGA was not a *State* organ.

The *Maffezini* tribunal stated, however, that the "structural test" was only one of the elements to be taken into consideration. The arbitrators noted that State enterprises may take many forms, and thus that the structural test by itself may not always lead to a conclusive determination as to whether an entity is an organ of the *State* or whether its acts may be attributed to the *State*. The arbitrators then referred to an additional functional test, one that examines the functions or the role to be performed by the entity.[50] In this regard, the *Maffezini* tribunal noted as follows:

"*This functional test has been applied, in respect of the definition of a national of a Contracting State, in the recent decision of an ICSID Tribunal on objections to jurisdiction in the case of* <u>Ceskoslovenska Obchodni Banka, A.S. v. the Slovak Republic</u>*. Here it was held that the fact of State ownership of the shares of the corporate entity was not enough to decide the crucial issue of whether the Claimant had standing under the Convention as a national of a Contracting State as long as the activities themselves were "essentially commercial rather than governmental in nature". By the same token, a private corporation operating for profit while discharging essentially governmental functions delegated to it by the State could, under the functional test, be considered as an organ of the State and thus engage the State's international responsibility for wrongful acts.*
It is difficult to determine, a priori, whether these various tests and standards need necessarily be cumulative. It is likely that there are circumstances when they need not be. Of

course, when all or most of the tests result in a finding of State action, the result, while still merely a presumption, comes closer to being conclusive."[51]

Under the "functional" test, the tribunal found that SODIGA had certain public powers and that it thus acted with certain delegated authority. To that extent, SODIGA's conduct was attributable to Spain.

The "structural" and "functional" tests for the purposes of determining jurisdiction *ratione personae* have also been used by other arbitration tribunals. In *Salini v. Morocco* the tribunal dealt with whether ADM, a commercial company with which foreign investors had negotiated the contract the performance of which had given rise to the dispute, was in fact a *State* company, and thus whether its actions could be attributed to the Kingdom of Morocco. The tribunal stated as follows:

"In order to determine the degree of control and participation of a State in a company, the Tribunal, referring to an ICSID award rendered in a case between Emilio Agustín Maffezini and the Kingdom of Spain (ICISD Case No.ARB/97/7) considers that it must take into account the international rules governing the liability of States. The assessment of the degree of State control and participation in a company is based on two criteria: the first, structural, in other words, related to the structure of the company and, in particular, to its shareholders; the other, functional, related to the objectives of the company in question."[52]

In *Salini v. Morocco* the tribunal found that from a structural point of view ADM was an entity controlled and managed by the Moroccan *State* through the intermediary of the Minister of Infrastructure, and that from a functional point of view ADM's main objective was to carry out tasks that were under *State* control, i.e. the *"building, managing and operating of assets under the province of the public utilities responding to the structural needs of the Kingdom of Morocco with regard to infrastructure and efficient communication networks"*.[53] On that ground, the tribunal concluded that from a structural and functional point of view ADM was an entity which was distinguishable from the *State* "solely on account of its legal personality", and thus that ADM was a *State* company acting in the name of the Kingdom of Morocco.

c. *Covered investments under IIAs and jurisdiction ratione materiae*

Another key variable in determining the jurisdiction *ratione materiae* of arbitral tribunals relates to the scope of application of the arbitration rules under which the ISDS proceedings are to be conducted.[54] While ad hoc arbitrations under some rules, such as those of UNCITRAL, grant practically total discretion to the parties to the dispute to agree on the kind of disputes that may be subject to ISDS procedures, Article 25 of the ICSID Convention provides for certain objective requirements which must be met for an ICSID tribunal to have jurisdiction to hear a particular case.

Thus, the jurisdiction of ICSID arbitral tribunals depends not only on the terms of the applicable IIA, but also on the specific requirements provided by Article 25 of the Convention. As will be explained below, although these two parameters for jurisdiction often coincide, this is not always the case. Furthermore, the jurisdiction *ratione materiae* of ISDS arbitral tribunals depends to a great extent on what is considered to be a covered "investment" under the IIA.

Over the last decade, jurisprudence has dealt with the different variables affecting the jurisdiction *ratione materiae* of ISDS arbitration tribunals. Most of the case law has developed in the context of the application of the ICSID Convention to treaty-based disputes, and it has tended to address three main questions. First, what kind of link must a covered investment have with the dispute so that Article 25(1) of the ICSID Convention can be applied? Second, which characteristics must be present so that a particular asset can be considered to be an "investment" subject to redress under ICSID procedures? The third question relates to the scope of ISDS mechanisms under some IIAs, and deals with the types of investment disputes that may be submitted to ISDS procedures, in particular claims related to contracts. The first two sets of issues will be explained below. The scope of ISDS mechanisms and the issues that arose regarding arbitral tribunals' jurisdiction over contract claims deserve particular attention and will be addressed in subsection d below.

(i) Link between the covered investment and the dispute

In most IIAs, the first clause of the ISDS provisions typically defines the types of disputes to which those mechanisms apply. Often, the mere existence of an investment is not enough for compliance with the requirements set out in some IIAs or applicable conventions in order to provide arbitral tribunals with jurisdiction *ratione materiae* to hear a case. Most IIAs require the existence of a link between the covered investment and the dispute. The most common approach used in IIAs is to provide that ISDS mechanisms shall apply to those disputes that in some way are related to a covered investment. Thus, some IIAs provide that ISDS procedures apply to those disputes that arise "*in connection with*" an investment, "*arising out*" of an investment, "*with respect to*" an investment, "*concerning*" an investment or "*related to*" an investment.[55] The nature of that link varies from one IIA to another, and its determination is not always an easy matter.

The relevance of this issue has been particularly important for cases submitted to ICSID, as Article 25 (1) of the ICSID Convention explicitly provides, inter alia, that the "[…] *jurisdiction of the Centre shall extend only to those* **legal disputes arising directly out of an investment**, *between a Contracting State* […] *and a national of another Contracting State* […]" (emphasis added).

Under that provision, for an arbitral tribunal to have jurisdiction *ratione personae* three elements are necessary. First, a dispute must exist; second, it has to be of a legal nature; and third, it must arise directly out of an investment. Although at first sight the requirement that a dispute exist may seem obvious,[56] it nevertheless has practical implications. It has been argued that the task of ICSID is to clarify legal questions *in abstracto*, handing down advisory or interpretative opinions like other international tribunals. Furthermore, it has been argued that the dispute between the parties involved must have some practical relevance; in this sense, the conflict should not be purely theoretical.[57]

The ICSID Convention, unlike the provisions of numerous clauses in IIAs, is not available for all kinds of disputes between an investor and the host country. Article 25 (1) explicitly states that for an ICSID arbitral tribunal to have jurisdiction, the dispute must be of a legal nature. In this regard, legal doctrine has stated that a dispute will qualify as legal only "[…] *if legal remedies such as restitution or damages are sought and if legal rights based on, for example, treaties or legislation are claimed*".[58] Over the last decade, neither of the latter two requirements has generated controversy in the context of ICSID cases, as most of the time both requirements are easily met when invoking the jurisdiction of the Centre. It is the third requirement, in Article 25 (1) of the Convention – the condition that the dispute must arise "*directly out of an investment*" – that has been addressed by some tribunals.

The first clarification regarding Article 25(1) of the ICSID Convention is that the requirement of "directness" contained therein relates to the link that must exist between the investment and the dispute, and does not relate to the kind of investment covered. In *FEDAX N.V. v. Venezuela*,[59] the respondent argued that the disputed transaction – six promissory notes issued by the Government of Venezuela – was not a "direct foreign investment" and therefore could not qualify as an "investment" under the Convention. The tribunal rejected that argument and noted:

> "[…] *It is apparent that the term "directly" relates in this Article to the "dispute" and not the "investment". It follows that jurisdiction can exist even in respect of investments that are not direct, so long as the dispute arises directly from such transaction.* […]"[60]

The issue of the directness of disputes in relation to the investment has frequently arisen in situations in which an investor has performed a series of transactions or contracts that are ancillary to the investment operation, and the dispute stems from compliance issues related to those transactions. In practice, it is difficult to distinguish between disputes arising directly out of an investment and those that have only an indirect link with the latter. The trend followed by ICSID arbitration tribunals has been to regard ancillary transactions that are vital to the investment as part of a "*general unity of an investment operation*".[61] Thus, disputes arising from those transactions, even if they have been conducted separately and carried out by means of different legal entities, have been regarded as fulfilling the requirement of directness set out in Article 25(1).[62] In this regard, in *Holiday Inns S.A. and others v. Morocco* the tribunal stated:

"*It is well known, and it is being particularly shown in the present case, that investment is accomplished by a number of juridical acts of all sorts. It would not be consonant either with economic reality or with the intention of the parties to consider each of these acts in complete isolation from the others. It is particularly important to ascertain which is the act which is the basis of the investment and which entails as measures of execution the other acts which have been concluded in order to carry it out.*"[63]

The fact that Article 25(1) of the ICSID Convention requires that the dispute arise directly out of an investment may have significant practical implications for the operation of several IIAs. As this requirement is an objective criterion for jurisdiction, it exists independently of the parties' consent – that is, irrespective of what the parties have agreed in the applicable IIA.

This raises potential problems with those IIAs that include extremely broad ISDS clauses. The latter state that, in principle, the ISDS procedures shall apply "*to every dispute between a Contracting Party and an investor of the other Party*". In those situations, a conflict arising between those parties that did not qualify according to Article 25 (1) of the ICSID Convention would have to be settled in accordance with possible other arbitration rules contained in the IIA. Although the prevailing trend in most IIAs is to provide investors with several alternative forums to adjudicate disputes, a number of IIAs provide only for the possibility of submitting an investment-related claim to ICSID, leaving investors with the domestic courts as the sole alternative choice.[64]

As stated before, the requirement that there be a link between the dispute and the investment – or measures relating to the investment – and the determination of the kind of link in order to provide an arbitral tribunal with jurisdiction also depend on the text of the applicable IIA. Over the last decade, this question has arisen in contexts different from those of ICSID cases. For instance, in *Methanex Corporation v. United States* – an UNCITRAL case under Chapter 11 of NAFTA – one of the issues was whether the measures complained of by the claimant actually were "*measures adopted or maintained by a Party relating to investors of another Party*", as provided by NAFTA's Article 1101. If the measures undertaken by the United States did not relate to Methanex, the case would have fallen outside the scope of application of NAFTA's chapter 11, and thus the arbitral tribunal would not have had jurisdiction.

Methanex was a Canadian investor that claimed compensation in the amount of approximately $970 million (together with interest and costs) from the United States, resulting from losses caused by the State of California's ban on the sale and use of the gasoline additive known as MTBE. Methanex was the world's largest producers of methanol, a feedstock for MTBE. However, it never produced or sold MTBE. Since none of the measures challenged was overtly aimed at methanol, methanol producers in general or Methanex in particular, the United States argued that the tribunal lacked jurisdiction, as the dispute did not involve a measure adopted or maintained by a Party – in this case, the United States – relating to investors of another Party – in this case, Methanex.

In its preliminary award on jurisdiction, the tribunal found that the term "relating to" in Article 1101 (1) of Chapter 11 required that there be a legally significant connection between the challenged measure and the investor. In this regard, the arbitral tribunal stated as follows:

"*We decide that the phrase "relating to" in Article 1101(1) NAFTA signifies something more than the mere effect of a measure on an investor or an investment and that it requires a legally significant connection between them [...] Pursuant to the rules of interpretation contained in Article 31(1) of the Vienna Convention, we base that decision upon the ordinary meaning of this phrase within its particular context and in the light of the particular object and purpose in NAFTA's Chapter 11 [...]."*[65]

On that basis, the arbitral tribunal found that Methanex's claim did not meet the essential requirement that it show facts establishing a legally significant connection between the United States measures, Methanex and its investments. The tribunal therefore decided that it had no jurisdiction to hear the claim. *Methanex* illustrates the relevance of the particular text used when drafting IIAs. Interestingly, the jurisdiction of the arbitration tribunal was determined on the basis of the scope of application of Chapter 11 as a whole, and not on the basis on the specific requirements set out in Section B of Chapter 11. The latter includes the ISDS provisions, which state that for a dispute to be submitted to arbitration, there needs to be a breach of an obligation in one of the provisions specified therein, with the investor having incurred loss or damage by reason of, or arising out of, that breach.

(ii) What is an investment?

Most BITs, traditionally aimed at the protection of investment, define "investment" in a way that is both broad and open-ended, covering not only the capital that has crossed the borders, but also practically all other kinds of assets invested by an investor in the territory of the host country. A significant number of BITs have included a standard definition of "investment", covering "*every kind of asset*" owned or controlled by an investor of another Party. This broad conceptualization of "investment" is typically complemented by an illustrative list of assets that are included within the definition. Such lists commonly include five categories of assets: movable and immovable property, interests in companies – including both portfolio and direct investment – contractual rights, intellectual property and business concessions.

The ICSID Convention does not define the term "investment". However, it has been interpreted broadly in ICSID practice and decisions. Over the years, arbitral tribunals have shown significant deference to what the contracting parties have agreed to consider covered investments in the IIA. Thus, a wide range of kinds of transactions – in the form not only of FDI, but also of portfolio investment – have fallen within the definition of "investment". The logic behind this approach is the assumption that the notion of "investment" has been left to the discretion of the parties in their framing of consent to arbitration.[66] Among the particular assets that arbitration tribunals have considered to be "investments" for the purposes of the ICSID Convention are shares in companies, public concession agreements, corporations organized under domestic law, loans, promissory notes, construction contracts, money spent in the renovation and development of a hotel, and the setting up of a law firm.[67]

The fact that traditionally the term "investment" has been broadly construed for the purposes of determining the jurisdiction of arbitral tribunals under Article 25(1) of the ICSID Convention should not lead to the conclusion that arbitral tribunals have given parties total discretion to decide what kind of investments they can submit to ICSID.

Over the last 10 years, several arbitration tribunals have stated that the term "investment" as used in Article 25(1) of the Convention has certain objective boundaries, which have to be respected in order to allow ICSID tribunals to have jurisdiction to hear a dispute. Three different cases seem to be particularly relevant regarding this question. The first is *FEDAX v. Venezuela*, which, according to the tribunal, was the first ICSID case in which the jurisdiction of the Centre was objected to on the ground that the underlying transaction did not meet the requirements of an "investment" under the Convention.[68]

This particular dispute was submitted by FEDAX, a company established under the laws of Curaçao, Netherlands Antilles, under the BIT between the Netherlands and Venezuela (1991). The claimant acquired, by way of endorsement, six promissory notes originally issued by Venezuela in connection with a contract concluded with a Venezuelan corporation. The main jurisdictional issue before the arbitral tribunal was whether the promissory notes held by FEDAX qualified as an "*investment*" within the meaning of Article 25(1) of the Convention.

The tribunal found that it had jurisdiction to hear the dispute, and based its reasoning on five main points. First, the tribunal noted that the ICSID Convention did not define the term "investment", thus leaving the definition to the discretion of the parties. Second, the tribunal drew attention to the fact that within this broad framework for the definition of "investment" under the ICSID Convention, a number of transactions such as loans, suppliers' credits, outstanding payments and ownership of shares had been identified as qualifying as "investments" in given circumstances. Third, the tribunal noted that loans qualify as an "investment" within ICSID jurisdiction, and that promissory notes are evidence of a loan and a rather typical financial credit instrument. Fourth, the tribunal considered that that the definition of "investment" in the BIT between the Netherlands and Venezuela comprised "*every kind of asset*", including "*titles to money, to other assets or to any performance having an economic value*". Fifth, the tribunal stated that:

> "[…] *A promissory note is by definition an instrument of credit, a written recognition that a loan has been made. In this particular case the six promissory notes in question were issued by the Republic of Venezuela in order to acknowledge its debt for the provision of services under a contract […] Venezuela had simply received a loan for the amount of the notes for the time period specified therein and with the corresponding obligation to pay interest.*"[69]

In *FEDAX v. Venezuela*, the tribunal respected to a significant degree the discretion of the parties in determining the meaning of the term "investment" for the purposes of Article 25(1) of the ICSID Convention. However, and to some extent in contradiction with the analytical approach used in their decision, the FEDAX arbitrators took an important step that could be further developed by future arbitral tribunals. For the first time, and in a subtle way, they made reference to certain objective criteria to define the term "investment" for the purposes of the ICSID Convention. In this regard, they stated as follows:

> "*The status of the promissory notes under the Law of Public Credit is also important as evidence that the type of investment involved is not merely a short-term, occasional financial arrangement, such as could happen with investments that come in for quick gains and leave immediately after – i.e. "volatile capital". The basic features of an investment have been described as involving a certain duration, a certain regularity of profit and return, assumption of risk, a substantial commitment and a significance for the host State development.* […]"[70]

After *FEDAX v. Venezuela*, another arbitral tribunal, in *Salini Costruttori S.p.A. and Italstrade S.p.A. v. Morocco*,[71] also favoured the approach towards an objective test for determining whether a particular transaction is an investment under Article 25(1) of the ICSID Convention. The dispute in *Salini v. Morocco* involved a contract for the construction of a highway, which was signed between two Italian companies and ADM, a Moroccan company controlled by the Kingdom of Morocco. The respondent objected to the jurisdiction of the tribunal on multiple grounds, one of which was that the contract in question did not constitute an "investment" within the meaning of the ICSID Convention.

While recognizing that the parties could, in principle, agree on the kind of disputes that could be submitted to the Centre, the tribunal went a step further than in *FEDAX* and explicitly recognized the existence of objective criteria that have to be met if a particular asset is to be considered an "investment" for the purposes of the ICSID Convention. The tribunal considered that its jurisdiction depended upon the existence of an "investment" within the meaning of the applicable IIA, in this case the BIT between Italy and Morocco (1990), but also on the basis of the ICSID Convention, in accordance with case law. Regarding the topic under discussion, the decision of the arbitral tribunal includes several paragraphs which are self-explanatory and worth quoting:

"*The Tribunal notes that there have been almost no cases where the notion of investment within the meaning of Article 25 of the Convention was raised. However, **it would be inaccurate to consider that the requirement that a dispute be "in direct relation to an investment" is diluted by the consent of the Contracting Parties**. To the contrary, ICSID case law and legal authors agree that the investment requirement must be respected as an objective condition of the jurisdiction of the Centre [...]*

The criteria to be used for the definition of an investment pursuant to the Convention would be easier to define if there were awards denying the Centre's jurisdiction on the basis of the transaction giving rise to the dispute. With the exception of a decision of the Secretary General of ICSID refusing to register a request for arbitration dealing with a dispute arising out of a simple sale [...] the awards at hand only very rarely turned on the notion of investment. Notably, the first decision only came in 1997 (Fedax case, cited above). The criteria for characterization are, therefore, derived from cases in which the transaction giving rise to the dispute was considered to be an investment without there ever being a real discussion on the issue in almost all the cases.

The doctrine generally considers that investment infers: contributions, a certain duration of performance of the contract and a participation in the risks of the transaction. In reading the Convention's preamble, one may add the contribution to the economic development of the host State of the investment as an additional condition.

*In reality, these various elements are independent. Thus, the risks of the transaction may depend on the contributions and the duration of performance of the contract. **As a result, these various criteria should be assessed globally**, even if, for the sake of reasoning, the Tribunal considers them individually here.*"[72] (emphasis added)

In *Salini v. Morocco*, the arbitral tribunal eventually concluded that the contract between ADM and the Italian companies constituted an "investment" in accordance with the terms of the BIT as well as Article 25 of the ICSID Convention. However, rather than focusing the analysis exclusively on the consent of the parties, the tribunal reached that conclusion only after testing whether the contract in question had met the overall objective criteria referred to above. In this regard, *Salini v. Morocco* represents a significant jurisprudential development.

The last step in the conceptual evolution of the meaning of the term "investment" under the ICSID Convention is the arbitral decision in *Joy Mining Machinery Limited v. Egypt*.[73] This was the first case in respect of which an ICSID arbitral tribunal concluded that it lacked jurisdiction because the transaction involved in the dispute did not qualify as an "investment" under Article 25 of the Convention.

In *Joy Mining v. Egypt*, a British company alleged that it had supplied mining equipment to an Egyptian State enterprise, IMC, for a project in Egypt under a contract requiring the claimant to put in place letters of guarantee. The claimant also alleged that although the equipment had been paid for, the guarantees were never released, and that it had been prevented by the Egyptian Government from carrying out the commissioning and performance testing of the equipment, which was a prerequisite for the release of the guarantees. Thus, the claimant sought damages for the full value of the bank guarantees not released, and argued that Egypt had violated its obligations under the BIT with the United Kingdom, in particular by expropriating and depriving Joy Mining of the returns on its investment and by failing to accord fair and equitable treatment and full protection and security. Among other objections to jurisdiction, Egypt argued that the bank guarantees could not be considered "investment" under the BIT and the ICSID Convention.

Adopting an objective approach to determining whether the transaction involved was a covered investment under the BIT, the tribunal concluded that the guarantees were merely a contingent liability and an ordinary feature of a sales contract and, therefore, not an "investment":

"[...] *To conclude that a contingent liability is an asset under Article 1(a) of the Treaty and hence a protected investment, would really go far beyond the concept of investment, even if broadly defined, as this and other treaties normally do.*"[74]

Referring to the FEDAX case, the claimant had argued that the guarantees fell within the definition of "investment" used in the BIT, which included "*claims to money or to any performance under contract having a financial value*". However, the tribunal was not persuaded by this argument, and stated as follows:

"[…] *Even if a claim to return of performance and related guarantees has a financial value it cannot amount to recharacterizing as an investment dispute a dispute which in essence concerns a contingent liability. The claim here is very different from that invoked in Fedax where the promissory notes held by the investor were the proceeds of an earlier credit transaction pursuant to which the State received value in exchange for its promise of future payment.*" [75]

Furthermore, after applying the same test as that used by the tribunal in *Salini v. Morocco*, the tribunal concluded that the guarantees did not possess the essential qualities to qualify as an "investment" under Article 25 of the ICSID Convention. Thus, ICSID jurisprudence on the term "investment" evolved from being an element on which the parties could basically freely agree to become an expression containing objective criteria:

"*The parties to a dispute cannot by contract or treaty define as investment, for the purpose of ICSID jurisdiction, something which does not satisfy the objective requirements of Article 25 of the Convention. Otherwise Article 25 and its reliance on the concept of investment, even if not specifically defined, would be turned into a meaningless provision [...].*"[76]

Furthermore, the tribunal in *Joy Mining v. Egypt*, following the reasoning in *FEDAX v. Venezuela* and *Salini v. Morocco*, consolidated the four requirements that, taken together, characterize an "investment":

"*Summarizing the elements that an activity must have in order to qualify as an investment, both the ICSID decisions mentioned above and the commentators thereon have indicated that the project in question should have a certain duration, a regularity of profit and return, an element of risk, a substantial commitment and that it should constitute a significant contribution to the host State's development. To what extent these criteria are met is of course specific to each particular case as they will normally depend on the circumstances of each case.*"[77]

The evolution of ICSID jurisprudence regarding the definition of "investment" under Article 25(1) of the Convention has significant practical implications for the negotiation and implementation of numerous IIAs. Despite the leeway that contracting parties have to agree on whatever definition of "investment" they may deem fit, not everything on which they concur might be considered "investment" under the ICSID Convention. This leads to the risk that disputes involving a covered investment under an IIA may not fall within the ICSID jurisdiction. This might force the parties to the dispute to attempt to adjudicate the conflict under other arbitration mechanisms. Perhaps the most significant outcome of this trend in ICSID jurisprudence is to make government officials reconsider whether the definition of "investment" included in numerous IIAs can lead to situations in which certain transactions that are not investments according to the above criteria may nevertheless fall within the scope of application of an agreement.

d. Investment treaty arbitration under IIAs and jurisdiction over contract claims

In most IIAs, the first clause of the ISDS provisions typically defines the types of disputes to which those mechanisms apply. The breadth of the scope of application of ISDS procedures varies significantly among IIAs. Some agreements provide for a broad scope of ISDS mechanisms and state that they shall apply to "*any dispute between a Contracting Party and an investor of the other Party*".[78] Other IIAs limit the scope of application of ISDS procedures, and provide that such mechanisms shall apply only to disputes "*concerning an alleged breach of an obligation under the Agreement which causes loss or damage to the investor or its investment.*"[79] The most common approach used in IIAs is to provide that ISDS mechanisms shall apply to those disputes that in some way are related to a covered investment. In this regard, some IIAs provide that ISDS mechanisms shall apply to those disputes which arise "*in connection with*" an investment, "*arising out*" of an investment, "*with respect to*" an investment, "*concerning*" an investment or "*related to*" an investment.

The determination of the scope of application of the ISDS mechanisms in IIAs has been one of the most debated topics in ISDS jurisprudence over the last decade. In particular, the debate has focused on whether the jurisdiction of an arbitral tribunal constituted under an IIA is limited to addressing breaches of substantive provisions of the agreement or whether the jurisdiction can be extended to address claims arising from breaches of an investment contract. This question has divided practitioners and legal commentators, and remains unsettled in ISDS jurisprudence.[80]

In order to place the discussion in its appropriate perspective, it may be useful to point out that over the last decade the issue of treaty claims versus contract claims has arisen in the context of numerous investment disputes. Very often these contracts have contained their own particular dispute settlement mechanisms under the domestic law of the host country. Thus, when investors have submitted contract claims to international arbitral tribunals, respondents have often objected to the jurisdiction of arbitral tribunals constituted under the applicable IIA on the ground that arbitrators have jurisdiction only to address claims related to breaches of the agreement.

Within that context, arbitral tribunals have been consistent in recognizing that a breach of a contract and a breach of the applicable IIA constitute separate causes for action.[81] However, recognizing the distinction between contract claims and treaty claims does not mean that an international arbitral tribunal never has jurisdiction to deal with claims arising under a contract. A careful discussion of the subject has to recognize that there are different factual situations in which an arbitral tribunal may deal with a claim based on an alleged breach of a contract. As a result, the legal analysis and consequences of establishing a contract breach may also lead to different outcomes. Each of these factual scenarios is analysed below.

(i) Situation in which a breach of a contract amounts to a breach of the IIA

It is uncontested in international investment jurisprudence that a violation of a contract can also entail a breach of a substantive obligation under an IIA. Thus, one can easily envisage a factual situation in which, by breaching a contract negotiated with an investor, the host country violates obligations typically included in most IIAs, such as the principle of fair and equitable treatment, or the commitment to refrain from discriminatory treatment of the investor or arbitrarily expropriating its property. For instance, in many cases, arbitral tribunals have held that measures undertaken by a State that have the effect of nullifying rights under a contract may amount to an expropriation.[82]

(ii) Situation in which only a breach of a contract is claimed

The situation in which an investor's claim is based solely on the breach of contract in the context of an arbitration tribunal constituted under an IIA is the one that has generated much debate in ISDS jurisprudence over the last decade. The fact that numerous ISDS clauses in IIAs provide that arbitration procedures may apply with regard to "*any*" or "*all*" disputes which arise "*in connection with*" or "*arising out*" of an investment has led to the question whether such language provides arbitration tribunals with jurisdiction to hear a claim based solely on an alleged breach of a contract – and not on a violation of the treaty itself. The ISDS jurisprudence over the last decade on this matter has not been uniform.

Some arbitration tribunals have provided that the dispute resolution clause is drafted in sufficiently broad language to extend to "*any*" or to "*all*" disputes assumed jurisdiction over mere contractual claims, including when the dispute relates to the performance of a contract. For instance, in *Salini v. Morocco*, Article 8 of the applicable IIA provided that the ISDS mechanisms applied to "*all disputes or differences*" between a contracting party and a covered investor.[83] Within this context, the tribunal found that:

> "*The terms of Article 8 are very general. The reference to expropriation and nationalisation measures, which are matters coming under the unilateral will of a State, **cannot be interpreted to exclude a claim based in contract from the scope of application of this Article**.*" (emphasis added)

Although it recognized its jurisdiction to hear mere contract claims, the tribunal introduced an important caveat. It read the ISDS clause as limiting the jurisdiction to all investment-related disputes between a covered investor and the *contracting party*, interpreting the latter part of the clause as limiting the jurisdiction of the tribunal to contracts in which the State itself, and not any other State entity, was a party.[84] The same approach was adopted by the arbitral tribunal in *Impregilo v. Pakistan*. In that case, the tribunal concluded that the scope of the dispute resolution clause in the BIT between Italy and Pakistan (1997) did not extend to breaches of a contract to which an entity other than the State was a party.[85]

Another example of an approach the favouring jurisdiction of arbitral tribunals over mere contractual claims is the decision of the ad hoc committee in *Vivendi I*. In this case, Article 8 of the BIT between France and Argentina (1991) included an ISDS clause applicable to "*any dispute relating to investments*". The committee stated as follows:

> "[…] *Article 8 deals generally with disputes "relating to investments made under this Agreement between one Contracting Party and an investor of the other Contracting Party."* […] *Article 8 does not use a narrower formulation, requiring that the investor's claim allege a breach of the BIT itself. Read literally, the requirements for arbitral jurisdiction in Article 8 do not necessitate that the Claimant allege a breach of the BIT itself: it is sufficient that the dispute relate to an investment made under the BIT. This may be contrasted, for example […] with Article 1116 of the NAFTA, which provides that an investor may submit to arbitration under Chapter 11 "a claim that another Party has breached and obligation under" specified provisions of that Chapter.*"[86]

Another case frequently cited in favour of recognizing the jurisdiction of arbitral tribunals over merely contractual claims when the ISDS provisions are sufficiently broad is *Société Générale de Surveillance S.A. (SGS) v. Philippines*. In that dispute, the applicable IIA was the BIT between Switzerland and the Philippines (1997), the ISDS provision of which applied to "*disputes with respect to investments*". The tribunal decided that the language used in the text of the IIA was general enough to allow the submission of all investment disputes, and that the term "*disputes*" was not limited by reference to the legal classification of the claim. Thus, the arbitrators found that the term included a dispute arising from an investment contract.[87]

In contrast to this arbitral decision, other arbitral tribunals have expressed the view that the broad wording of the ISDS provision in an IIA is not sufficient to establish jurisdiction with regard to purely contractual claims. One of the frequently cited cases favouring this approach involves the same Swiss company in a dispute with Pakistan. In *Société Générale de Surveillance S.A. (SGS) v. Pakistan*[88] the tribunal stated as follows:

"We recognize that disputes arising from claims grounded on alleged violations of the BIT, and disputes arising from claims based wholly on supposed violations of the PSI Agreement, can both be described as "disputes with respect to investments", the phrase used in Article 9 of the BIT. That phrase, however, while descriptive of <u>the factual subject matter of the disputes</u>, does not relate to the <u>legal basis</u> of the claims, or the <u>cause of action</u> asserted in the claims. In other words, from that description alone, without more, we believe that no implication necessarily arises that both BIT and purely contract claims are intended to be covered by the Contracting Parties in Article 9. […] Thus, we do not see anything in Article 9 or in any other provision of the BIT that can be read as vesting this Tribunal with jurisdiction over claims resting <u>ex hypothesi</u> exclusively on contract […] We are not suggesting that the parties cannot, by special agreement, lodge in this Tribunal jurisdiction to pass upon and decide claims sounding solely in the contract. Obviously the parties can. But we do not believe that they have done so in this case. And should the parties opt to do that, our jurisdiction over such contract claims will rest on the special agreement, not on the BIT."[89]

On the basis of this reasoning, the tribunal in *SGS v. Pakistan* found that it lacked jurisdiction with respect to claims based on alleged breaches of contract that did not amount to breaches of the substantive obligations in the BIT. Another, more recent occasion on which an arbitral tribunal emphasized the requirement that contract claims submitted to treaty-based arbitration should also constitute a breach of an obligation of the treaty was in *Consorzio Groupement L.E.S.I. DIPENTA v. Algeria.*[90] In that dispute the claimant relied on the broad scope of the ISDS provision contained in Article 8(1) of the BIT between Algeria and Italy (1991). The tribunal held as follows:

"Nevertheless, the fact that the Respondent has given its written consent does not necessarily mean that such consent is general in scope and that it establishes the basis of jurisdiction for any violation that the Claimant might invoke. The consent given holds only as far as the Bilateral Agreement allows. […] It may be concluded that the consent was not given in an extensive way for all claims and actions that might be related to an investment. The measures taken must amount to a breach of the Bilateral Agreement, which means in particular that they must be unjustified or discriminatory, in fact or in law. That is not necessarily the case with every breach of contract."[91]

The case law referred to above shows that there is not a uniform trend in ISDS jurisprudence regarding whether a broadly drafted dispute settlement clause in an IIA may be sufficient to grant jurisdiction to arbitral tribunals to hear purely contractual-based claims. However, the discussion takes a different direction when the applicable IIA includes an "umbrella clause". This situation is discussed below.

(iii) Situation in which the IIA includes an "umbrella clause"

A third factual scenario in which a tribunal may deal with contract claims in the context of an investment dispute is when the applicable IIA includes an umbrella clause. This is a provision frequently included in BITs under which the contracting parties undertake to comply with any obligation they have assumed with respect to investments (UNCTAD 2007, p. 73). Article 11 of the BIT between Switzerland and the Pakistan (1995) illustrates this kind of provision, and reads as follows:

"Either Contracting Party shall constantly guarantee the observance of the commitments it has entered into with respect to the investments of the investors of the other Contracting Party."

In international legal doctrine it is widely accepted that through the effect of an umbrella clause, a breach of a contract becomes a treaty violation.[92] However, ISDS jurisprudence has not been consistent regarding the effect of the umbrella clauses over the last decade. While some arbitral tribunals have agreed with most of the international legal doctrine, others have rejected the argument that umbrella clauses have the effect of elevating breaches of contract to a violation of the applicable agreement.

In this regard, five disputes are particularly relevant: *SGS v. Pakistan*,[93] *Joy Mining v. Egypt*,[94] *SGS v. Philippines*,[95] *L.E.S.I-DIPENTA v. Algeria*[96] and *Eureko B.V. v. Poland*.[97] While in the first two arbitral tribunals, in their respective specific factual scenarios, rejected the view that umbrella clauses have the effect of transforming all contract disputes into treaty disputes under the applicable agreement, arbitrators held the opposite view in the other three cases.

The reasons for limiting the effect of the umbrella clauses have been different. For instance, in *SGS v. Pakistan* – which according to the tribunal was the first international tribunal to examine the legal effect of an umbrella clause in a BIT – the arbitral tribunal argued that the effects of an umbrella clause were potentially so sweeping that evidence was needed to demonstrate that those effects were in fact intended by the contracting parties to the BIT:

> "*Considering the widely accepted principle with which we started, namely, that under general international law, a violation of a contract entered into by a State with an investor of another State, is not, by itself, a violation of international law, and considering further that* **the legal consequences that the Claimant would have us attribute to Article 11 of the BIT are so far-reaching in scope, and so automatic and unqualified and sweeping in their operation, so burdensome in their potential impact upon a Contracting Party, we believe that clear and convincing evidence must be adduced by the Claimant.** *Clear and convincing evidence of what? Clear and convincing evidence* **that such was indeed the shared intent of the Contracting Parties to the Swiss-Pakistan Investment Protection Treaty** *in incorporating Article 11 in the BIT. We do not find such evidence in the text itself of Article 11. We have not been pointed to any other evidence of the putative common intent of the Contracting Parties by the Claimant.*" (emphasis added)[98]

In *Joy Mining v. Egypt*, the arbitral tribunal also rejected the view that an umbrella clause has the effect of converting any contract claim into a treaty claim. However, in this particular case, the transactions which were the basis for the dispute were bank guarantees that were found by the tribunal to be simply a contingent liability and not "investments" for the purposes of Article 25(1) of the ICSID Convention. Thus, unlike in *SGS v. Pakistan*, the position of the arbitral tribunal in *Joy Mining v. Egypt* was not to comment on whether an umbrella clause would have the effect of transforming a claim based on an investment contract into a treaty claim. Rather, the tribunal considered that in a situation where a contract is not an investment, the latter could not be converted into a covered investment by virtue of an umbrella clause:

> "*In this context, it could not be held that an umbrella clause inserted in the Treaty, and not very prominently, could have the effect of transforming all contract disputes into investment disputes under the Treaty, unless of course there would be a clear violation of the Treaty rights and obligations or a violation of contract rights of such a magnitude as to trigger the Treaty protection, which is not the case. The connection between the Contract and the Treaty is the missing link that prevents any such effect. This might be perfectly different in other cases where that link is found to exist, but certainly it is not the case here.*"[99]

In *SGS v. Philippines*, the dispute concerned a contract concluded between SGS and the Philippines regarding the provision of comprehensive import supervision services (the CISS Agreement), under which SGS would provide specialized services to assist in improving the customs clearance and control processes of the Philippines. The dispute arose between the parties as a result of alleged breaches of the CISS Agreement. SGS invoked the BIT between Switzerland and the Philippines (1997). Article X(2) of that treaty states as follows:

"Each Contracting Party shall observe any obligation it has assumed with regard to specific investments in its territory by investors of the other Contracting Party."

In *SGS v. Philippines*, the interpretation of the umbrella clause cited above was radically different from that in *SGS v. Pakistan*. After making a subtle criticism of the reasoning of the latter, and stating that it *"failed to give any clear meaning to the umbrella clause"*, the tribunal found that "[…] *Article X(2) makes it a breach of the BIT for the host State to fail to observe binding commitments, including contractual commitments, which it has assumed with regard to specific investments"*.[100] However, the arbitration tribunal interpreted the umbrella clause in the BIT and the contract in a systematic manner. In this regard, the tribunal noted as follows:

"Article X(2) includes commitments or obligations arising under contracts entered into by the host State. The basic obligation on the State in this case is the obligation to pay what is due under the contract, which is an obligation assumed with regard to the specific investment (the performance of services under the CISS Agreement). But this obligation does not mean that the determination of how much money the Philippines is obliged to pay becomes a treaty matter. The extent of the obligation is still governed by the contract, and it can only be determined by reference to the terms of the contract."[101]

In addition to *SGS v. Philippines*,[102] the arbitral tribunal in *L.E.S.I-DIPENTA v. Algeria* explicitly stated that the effect of the umbrella clauses "[…] *is to transform breaches of the State's contractual commitments into violations of that provision of the treaty and, accordingly, to endow the arbitral tribunal constituted in accordance with the treaty with jurisdiction* [over such breaches]".[103] Furthermore, a more recent decision reached the same conclusion. In *Eureko B.V. v. Poland* contractual arrangements between the investor and the host country were subject to the jurisdiction of the tribunal pursuant to the application of the umbrella clause included in the 1992 BIT between the Netherlands and Poland.

e. *Litis pendens* and "fork-in-the-road" clauses

During the last decade, some IIAs have included provisions that prevent a particular investment dispute from being addressed in more than one dispute settlement forum, with the host country being required to respond to the same claims more than once and with the possibility of inconsistent decisions. Of special concern is the possibility that the investor may submit a dispute to the domestic courts of the host country and simultaneously or subsequently submit the same dispute to international arbitration.

Two approaches have been used in IIAs to deal with this issue. Some agreements force the investor to decide, *ab initio*, whether the dispute shall be adjudicated in domestic tribunals or through international arbitration. Once the dispute is submitted to either forum, the election shall be definitive. An example of this technique – known in treaty practice as the "fork-in-the-road" provision – is illustrated by Article IX.3 of the BIT between Indonesia and Chile (1999), which provides that:

"Once the investor has submitted the dispute to the competent tribunal of the Contracting Party in whose territory the investment was made or to international arbitration, that election shall be final."

The other approach used by some IIAs – known as the "no-U-turn" – is to provide the investor with the possibility of making a final decision on the venue for solving the dispute at a later stage, even after the investor has submitted the dispute to the administrative or judicial tribunals of the host country. IIAs applying this technique allow the investor to opt for international arbitration as long as domestic tribunals have not rendered a final judgement. Article XIII.3 of the BIT between Canada and Thailand (1997) illustrates this approach, and provides that an investor may submit a dispute to arbitration only if:

"[…] *the investor has waived to initiate or continue any other proceedings in relation to the measure that is alleged to be in breach of this Agreement before the courts or tribunals of the Contracting Party concerned or in a dispute settlement procedure of any kind.*"

Despite their different wording, both approaches referred to above attempt to prevent the same investment dispute from being addressed in more than one forum at the same time (*litis pendens*). On the other hand, ISDS jurisprudence over the last decade clearly shows that the particular wording of specific clauses does matter and can make a difference. Indeed, ISDS jurisprudence regarding these two different approaches has led to different practical results.

In *Waste Management Inc. v. Mexico*,[104] an arbitration procedure conducted under ICSID's Additional Facility Rules, the arbitral tribunal interpreted NAFTA's Article 1121 (Conditions Precedent to Submission of a Claim to Arbitration). Article 1121 is an example of a "no-U-turn" approach, and states in its relevant part as follows:

"*1. **A disputing investor may submit a claim under Article 1116 to arbitration only if:** [...] **(b) the investor** and, where the claim is for loss or damage to an interest in an enterprise of another Party that is a juridical person that the investor owns or controls directly or indirectly, the enterprise, **waive their right to initiate or continue before any administrative tribunal or court under the law of any Party**, or to other dispute settlement procedures, **any procedures with respect to the measure** of the disputing Party **that is alleged to be a breach** referred to in Article 1116, except for proceedings for injunctive, declaratory or other extraordinary relief, not involving the payment of damages, before an administrative tribunal or court under the law of the disputing Party.*" (emphasis added)

In *Waste Management v. Mexico*, one of the issues addressed by the tribunal was whether, after the establishment of the arbitral tribunal, the continuation of the proceedings initiated by the investors' subsidiary, Acaverde, in Mexican courts fell within the prohibition of NAFTA Article 1121 in that they address measures that were also invoked in the arbitral proceedings as breaches of NAFTA provisions. The arbitral tribunal found that this was the case, and that, consequently, the investor did not comply with the requirements set out in NAFTA's Article 1121(2)(b):

"[…] *In effect, it is possible to consider that proceedings instituted in a national forum may exist which do not relate to those measures alleged to be in violation of the NAFTA by a member state of the NAFTA, in which case it would be feasible that such proceedings could coexist simultaneously with an arbitration proceeding under the NAFTA. **However, when both legal actions have a legal basis derived from the same measures, they can no longer continue simultaneously in light of the imminent risk that the Claimant may obtain the double benefit in its claim for damages**. This is precisely what NAFTA Article 1121 seeks to avoid. [...]*"[105] (emphasis added)

Given the particular language used in NAFTA's Article 1121, the identity of the measure challenged by the investor in both domestic courts and the arbitration process led the tribunal in *Waste Management v. Mexico* to hold that it lacked jurisdiction to hear the dispute.

In other contexts, disputes in which the applicable IIA contain a "fork-in-the-road" clause have led to very different practical results. Over the last decade, one of the issues addressed relatively frequently in the ISDS jurisprudence has been whether a foreign investor's or its local subsidiary's appearance before local courts triggers the "fork-in-the-road" clause included in some IIAs. This has been the issue in several cases brought against Argentina in the wake of that country's financial crisis.

For instance, in *CMS Gas Transmission Company v. Argentina*[106] the respondent argued that CMS had triggered the fork-in-the-road provision when CMS's subsidiary, TGN, appealed before the local courts against the judicial injunction concerning an adjustment to the fees of the contract involved.

Making reference to a series of previous cases, such as *Alex Genin, Eastern Credit Limited v. Estonia*,[107] *Compañia de Aguas del Aconquija & Vivendi Universal v. Argentina*[108] and *Eudoro Olguin v. Paraguay*,[109] the tribunal distinguished between contractual and treaty claims, and held as follows:

> "[...] *as contractual claims are different from treaty claims, even if there had been or there currently was a recourse to the local courts for breach of contract, this would not have prevented submission of the treaty claims to arbitration. This Tribunal is persuaded that with even more reason this view applies to the instant dispute, since no submission has been made by CMS to local courts and since, even if TGN had done so – which is not the case –, this would not result in triggering the "fork-in-the-road" provision against CMS.* **Both the parties and the causes of action under separate instruments are different.**"[110] (emphasis added)

ISDS jurisprudence has tended to converge regarding this particular matter. In many instances, arbitral tribunals made reference to the award in *S.A.R.L. Benvenuti & Bonfant v. Congo*, where the tribunal held that there is *litis pendens* only if there is "*identity of the parties, object and cause of action in the proceeding pending before two or more tribunals*".[111] Arbitral tribunals have rarely found this "fork-in-the-road" provision to apply in disputes brought before domestic tribunals and in international arbitration proceedings.

In sum, using the reasoning used in *CMS v. Argentina*, several recent arbitral tribunals have refrained from applying the "fork-in-the-road" provisions existing in IIAs on the basis of the following elements. First, arbitrators have tended to differentiate between those claims based on the treaty – treaty claims – and those having their origin in contracts – contract claims. Second, arbitrators have distinguished between the legal personality of the investor – usually the claimant – and the legal personality of the investor's subsidiaries, which are typically are parties to the contracts concerned. Third, as *litis pendens* exists only where there is identity of *parties, object and cause of action,* it follows that there will be jurisdiction if the causes of action or the formal identity of the parties in the arbitration proceedings are not the same as those of the parties in the domestic courts.

In addition to the cases already referred to, this reasoning has been applied in disputes such as *Azurix Corp. v. Argentina*,[112] *Enron and Ponderosa Assets v. Argentina*[113] and *LG&E v. Argentina*.[114] This has a series of practical consequences.

Since several arbitral decisions have interpreted the "fork-in-the-road" provision as resulting in a loss of access to international arbitration only where the dispute and the parties are identical,[115] it is easy to envisage a situation in which a shareholder initiates arbitration to protect its rights under an IIA, while the investment (i.e. the subsidiary) initiates a domestic dispute to protect its contract or other legal rights, including those stemming from the IIA. Furthermore, under the prevailing interpretation of "fork-in-the-road" provisions, one can also easily imagine situations in which an investor may submit a claim under ISDS procedures despite the existence of a "domestic forum" clause in an investment contract between the investor and the host country. This would be possible, since the "domestic forum" clause would relate only to breaches of the contract, while the investor–State claim relates to violations of the treaty itself as a separate international obligation.[116]

2. Matters related to the conduct of the dispute settlement process

a. *Consolidation of proceedings*

Given the multiplicity of existing IIAs, and considering that the same set of measures implemented by the host country may affect numerous foreign investors, it is not uncommon that the same facts and circumstances are litigated by different investors in different tribunals. The contradictory outcomes in the Lauder cases are often cited as an illustration of this potential problem.[117] In those disputes, two different arbitration tribunals held that parallel proceedings relating to the same facts were admissible on the ground that nominally the parties and the two BITs involved were different.[118] The Lauder cases have illustrated the risk of lack of finality in a given investment dispute, leading to the possibility that host countries could lose arbitration proceedings several times and thus be subject to multiple awards.

Most IIAs lack specific provisions addressing the possibility of consolidating different disputes arising from the same set of facts or measures. Given that under arbitration proceedings the parties to the dispute enjoy considerable discretion to agree on procedural matters, nothing would in principle prevent them from agreeing consolidate two or more disputes into a single proceeding. However, once a dispute is submitted to arbitration, the acrimony between the parties involved in the dispute may inhibit them from agreeing on this kind of procedure.

The potential problem of having multiple proceedings for the same set of facts was foreseen in the context of NAFTA's Chapter 11, where Articles 1117.3 and 1126 authorize tribunals to consolidate disputes under certain circumstances. Article 1126.2 grants a certain degree of discretion to the tribunals to determine whether to proceed with the consolidation of disputes. However, this provision also specifies that four requirements are necessary for a tribunal to be able to consolidate. First, all claims must have been submitted to arbitration in accordance with the requirements set forth in NAFTA's Article 1120. Second, the claims must have a "question of law or fact in common". Third, the consolidation should be executed "in the interests of fair and efficient resolution of the claims", and fourth, consolidation may proceed only "after hearing the disputing parties".

In the context of the application of NAFTA's Chapter 11, there have so far been two attempts at consolidation of claims. In the first case, Mexico requested the establishment of a tribunal to consider the consolidation of two disputes, *Corn Products International, Inc. v. Mexico*[119] and *Archer Daniels Midland Company & Tate & Lyle Ingredients Americas Inc. v. Mexico*.[120] Both disputes concerned an excise tax on certain soft drinks. Mexico's request for consolidation was strongly resisted by the claimants, who argued that consolidation would not be in the interest of a fair and efficient resolution of the claims because they were market competitors. The consolidation tribunal considered that although Mexico had argued "*with persuasive force*" that the claims submitted by the two investors were very much the same, the consolidation should not proceed on the ground that the investors involved were in "*fierce*" and direct competition. In this regard, the tribunal stated as follows:

> "*The direct and major competition between the claimants, and the consequent need for complex confidentiality measures throughout the arbitration process, would render consolidation in this case, in whole or in part, extremely difficult. The parties would not be in a position to work together and share information. The process, including essential confidentiality agreements, discovery, written submissions and oral arguments would have to be carried out, in substantial measure, on separate tracks. The consolidation of the claims of direct and major competitors would necessarily result in complex and slow proceedings in order to protect the confidentiality of sensitive information. [...] **Under such circumstances, a consolidation order cannot be in the interests of fair and efficient resolution of the claims**. Two tribunals can handle two separate cases more fairly and efficiently than one tribunal where the two claimants are direct and major competitors, and the claims raise issues of competitive and commercial sensitivity. [...] [Furthermore] the **Tribunal is persuaded that notwithstanding certain common questions of fact and law, the numerous distinct issues of state responsibility and quantum further confirm the need for separate proceedings**.*"[121] (emphasis added)

The second consolidation attempt led to a different result. It involved a request by the United States to consolidate three softwood lumber cases, *Canfor Corp. v. United States of America*, *Terminal Forest Products Ltd. v. United States of America* and *Tembec Inc. et al. v. United States of America*.[122] As in the previous case, the claimants strongly objected to the consolidation of the disputes; however, in the end, the consolidation request succeeded. Unlike the consolidation tribunal in *Corn Products*, in *Canfor* the tribunal examined in detail the meaning of the requirements for consolidations set forth in NAFTA's

Article 1126, and in particular what should be understood by "*a question of law or fact in common*". In this regard, the tribunal stated as follows:

> "*The notion of "question" in the term "a question of law or fact in common" [...] means a factual or legal issue that requires a finding to dispose of a claim. [...] An issue to which the invocation of a provision of Section A of Chapter 11 of the NAFTA gives rise, should, therefore, be in common in the Article 1120 arbitrations. The mere invocation of the same provision of the NAFTA is not sufficient. [...]*
> *Furthermore, a fact may be in common in the Article 1120 arbitrations, but here again there should also be an issue concerning that fact that is in common. [...]*
> *Another question is whether one or several questions of law or fact are necessary to justify an order under Article 1126(2). [...] the presence of one common question of either law or fact in two or more Article 1120 arbitrations will serve that object and purpose under given circumstances. [...] the question need not be purely a quantitative one, but a qualitative one as well. The determination that one question of law or fact is in common, requires a further determination that resolution of that question is in the interests of fair and efficient resolution of the claims. Thus, at least one question of law or fact in common may present itself, but resolution of that question by an Article 1126 Tribunal may not serve the fair and efficient resolution of the claims advanced before the Article 1120 Tribunals. Whether that is so depends entirely on the circumstances of the cases and cannot be answered in the abstract.*"[123]

After developing its understanding of the concept of "*common questions of law or fact*" as used in Article 1126 (2) of the NAFTA, the consolidation tribunal concluded in *Canfor* that the proceedings before it met the four conditions included in that provision.[124] Furthermore, it made an effort to explain why its decision in favour of consolidation resulted from a situation that was different from the one in *Corn Products*.[125]

b. Transparency

Under most arbitration systems, the existence of a dispute, its documents and pleadings, and often its decisions, are not made public. This is because the ISDS system is based on international commercial arbitration, which came into existence as a tool for the settling of international commercial disputes between private parties, mainly on technical legal grounds not involving public policy issues. While confidentiality in private disputes is warranted, this may not be the case when arbitral tribunals rule on matters of broad public concern that can arise in connection with a major investment project by host countries.

ISDS disputes frequently involve matters that have a greater public impact than is typically the case in disputes between particular private actors, because the State is involved and measures implemented by the host Government are challenged. The increase in the number of investment disputes and the fact that both capital-importing and capital-exporting countries have become respondents in ISDS proceedings have enhanced the visibility of – and often the controversy surrounding – IIAs in general and ISDS in particular as regards domestic and international public opinion. As a result, demands are increasingly being made for greater openness and transparency of arbitral processes.

An overview of ISDS experience regarding the issue of transparency should differentiate between the topic in the general context of ISDS arbitration and in the context of NAFTA's Chapter 11 cases. It is in the NAFTA context that the pressure for the fostering of transparency and greater participation by civil society in ISDS has been greatest; also, the most significant developments in the evolution of investment rulemaking have taken place in connection with NAFTA.

In the context of general ISDS experience, there have been efforts over the last decade to increase the transparency of investor–State disputes. For instance, ICSID has produced a web-based list of its past and current cases,[126] and a party to ICSID proceedings has always had the right to release awards and other decisions into the public domain unilaterally unless there was an agreement between the parties to the contrary. Furthermore, the ICSID secretariat has the authority to publish significant extracts from decisions where the parties do not agree to publish an award. The recent proposals for the review of ICSID procedures suggest that although *"the Centre shall not publish the award without the consent of the parties, the Centre shall, however, promptly include in its publications excerpts of the legal reasoning of the Tribunal"*.[127]

Despite these efforts, it remains a fact that under ICSID the degree of transparency of the ISDS process depends to a great extent on the agreement of the parties to the dispute. This situation leaves arbitral tribunals with very limited authority to foster greater transparency and participation by civil society in ISDS proceedings. An illustration is the recent case *Aguas del Tunari S.A. v. Bolivia*.[128]

This dispute, submitted to ICSID, involved a concession contract between the city of Cochabamba and Aguas del Tunari, a Bolivian company controlled by Dutch investors. The claimants alleged that Bolivia, through various acts and omissions leading up to, and including, the rescission of the concession, breached various provisions of the BIT between Bolivia and the Netherlands (1992).

In the early stages of the proceedings, an environmental non-governmental organization (NGO) filed a petition with the tribunal requesting permission to intervene in the arbitration. In particular, the petitioners asked the tribunal to grant them standing and afford them all rights of participation accorded to other parties. First, they should be allowed to make submissions regarding the jurisdiction, procedural matters and substantive aspects of the dispute. Second, they should have the right to attend all hearings of the tribunal. Third, they should be entitled to make oral presentations during the hearings. Fourth, they should have access to all submissions made to the tribunal. In addition, the petitioners requested the tribunal to publicly disclose all statements and submissions concerning the claims and defenses of both parties to the dispute, open all hearings to the public and visit the area of Cochamba, Bolivia, where the contract was to be executed.

The President of the tribunal wrote a letter to the petitioners indicating that, after considering their requests and the views of the parties to the dispute, it observed the following:

"[T]he Tribunal's unanimous opinion [is] *that your core requests are beyond the power of the authority of the Tribunal to grant. The interplay of the two treaties involved (the Convention on the Settlement of Investment Disputes and the 1992 Bilateral Agreement on Encouragement and Reciprocal Protection of Investments between the Kingdom of the Netherlands and Bolivia) and the consensual nature of arbitration places the control of the issues you raise with the parties, not the Tribunal. In particular, it is manifestly clear to the Tribunal that it does not, absent the agreement of the Parties, have the power to join a non-party to the proceedings; to provide access to hearings to non parties and, a fortiori, to the public generally; or to make the documents of the proceedings public."*[129]

The tribunal's letter also acknowledges that the parties to the dispute did not consent to grant the requests, and that *"[a]lthough the Tribunal did not receive any indication that such consent may be forthcoming, the Tribunal remains open to any initiative from the parties in this regard."*[130]

Regarding the possibility of allowing the petitioners to participate as *amicus curiae*, the tribunal considered that there was no need at that moment to call witnesses or seek supplementary non-party submissions, because it was still examining its jurisdiction. However, the tribunal left the door open to accepting *amicus curiae* participation in the later stages of the dispute.[131]

This last statement by the tribunal is important, as it confirms its authority to call witnesses or receive information from non-parties during the ISDS proceedings. Thus, despite the fact that the degree of transparency of the ISDS process under ICSID depends, to a great extent, on the agreement of the parties to the dispute, the tribunal seems to suggest that non-parties to the dispute might still be admitted to the proceedings through the submission of *amicus curiae* briefs or, if applicable, being called as witnesses. This approach follows the emerging practice in State-to-State dispute settlement procedures at the World Trade Organization (WTO), where it has gradually been accepted that NGOs may submit *amicus curiae* briefs for consideration by the panels.

The ISDS practice on transparency in the NAFTA context is illustrative in many ways. Not only has NAFTA's ISDS jurisprudence on transparency been more prolific, but also the NAFTA experience is an interesting example of how ISDS practice can have a significant impact on investment rulemaking regarding this particular issue.

Since the entry into force of NAFTA in 1994, the ISDS experience regarding transparency can be divided in two periods, the dividing line between them being 31 July 2001 – the date on which the NAFTA Free Trade Commission enacted the Notes of Interpretation of Certain Chapter 11 Provisions. Among other important substantive clarifications, these Notes clarified certain provisions of the agreement affecting the transparency of ISDS proceedings.

Prior to the Free Trade Commission's Decision of 2001, arbitral tribunals had tended to interpret the applicable arbitration provisions in such a way as to increase transparency in ISDS proceedings. Since neither Canada nor Mexico is a Contracting State of the ICSID Convention, the ISDS jurisprudence under NAFTA on transparency has focused on the interpretation of the UNCITRAL rules or ICSID's Additional Facility Rules. Greater transparency has been sought through three different methods: first, disclosure of documents; second, allowing non-party participation in the form of *amicus curiae* briefs; and third, opening the hearings in the disputes.

The issue of transparency has been discussed in a number of NAFTA ISDS proceedings. For instance, in *Metalclad Corporation v. the United Mexican States* the arbitration tribunal noted that neither the NAFTA nor the ICSID Additional Facility Rules contain any express limit on the parties' freedom to publicize information divulged during the arbitration.[132] Furthermore, in *Loewen v. United States* the tribunal stated that a general duty of confidentiality in arbitration involving a State party would be undesirable, as it would restrict public access to information relating to government and public matters.[133]

However, it was in the context of two other cases, namely *Methanex v. United States*[134] and *UPS v. Canada*[135] that arbitral tribunals were called upon to decide on concrete transparency-related matters.

In *Methanex v. United States*, a dispute governed by the UNCITRAL arbitration rules, the arbitral tribunal had before it a petition by several NGOs requesting that they be allowed, first, to file *amicus* briefs; second, to review the parties' written pleadings; third, to make written and oral submissions; and fourth, to participate in the oral hearings.

As a starting point, the arbitral tribunal noted that Article 15(1) of the UNCITRAL arbitration rules empowers a tribunal to conduct the proceedings between the parties in such manner, as it deems appropriate, provided that the parties are treated on the basis of equality:

"*Article 15(1) is intended to provide the broadest procedural flexibility within fundamental safeguards, to be applied by the arbitration tribunal to fit the particular needs of the particular arbitration. As procedural provision, however, it cannot grant the Tribunal any power to add further disputing parties to the arbitration, nor to accord to persons who are non-parties the substantive status, rights or privileges of a Disputing Party. Likewise, the Tribunal can have no power to accord to any third person the substantive rights of NAFTA Parties under Article 1128 of NAFTA. The issue is whether Article 15(1) grants the Tribunal any lesser procedural power in regard to non-party third persons, such as the Petitioners here.*"

Within that logic, the *Methanex* tribunal noted that neither NAFTA's Chapter 11 nor the UNICTRAL Arbitration Rules include express powers allowing or prohibiting the acceptance of *amicus* briefs. The tribunal concluded that by virtue of Article 15(1) of the UNCITRAL Arbitration Rules, it had the power to accept *amicus curiae* submissions in writing, provided that they were copied simultaneously to the legal representatives of the disputing parties, Canada and Mexico. Further, the tribunal considered that it had no power to grant the NGOs' requests to receive materials generated within the arbitration or to attend oral hearings of the arbitration. As the parties did not agree to the disclosure of confidential information with the exception of the standard disclosure of major pleadings, orders and awards of the tribunal, the information had to remain confidential.

Regarding the possibility of holding hearings open to the public, the tribunal determined in *Methanex v. United States* that Article 25(4) of the UNCITRAL Arbitration Rules, which provides for in-camera hearings, prevents it from allowing the presence of third parties at the oral hearings without party consent. However, both parties to the dispute decided to make the hearings public.

In *UPS v. Canada* the arbitral tribunal relied on *Methanex* to a great extent. It also determined that it had the power to allow third party participation through the submission of *amicus* briefs. Drawing upon the *Methanex* reasoning and decision, the tribunal stated that Article 15(1) of the UNCITRAL Arbitration Rules granted it the power to conduct the arbitration in such manner, as it deemed appropriate. Regarding the possibility of attending hearings or receiving documents generated in the arbitration process, the tribunal relied on Article 25(4) to exclude any prospect of third party attendance at the hearings, which in the absence of consensus between the parties, would be held in camera. As in *Methanex*, both the hearings and the written arguments were finally made public with the agreement of the parties.

It follows from the above that the principle of transparency has been mostly promoted in the context of NAFTA's Chapter 11. The latter provides for public notification of new disputes, and its arbitration process has become increasingly open over the past several years. In line with the interpretative statement by NAFTA's Free Trade Commission,[136] the websites of the three NAFTA parties now provide routine access to notices of arbitration, claims and counterclaims, memorials, procedural decisions, and substantive decisions and awards.

C.   Interpretation of IIAs: Substantive issues

In this section, the main substantive legal grounds for awards in the cases under review are examined. They are highly important as authoritative interpretations of the substantive obligations contained in IIA provisions. IIAs are dynamic instruments that evolve over time to meet the needs of investment protection, on the one hand, and the flexibility of host countries to regulate economic activity, on the other hand. In these circumstances, a major task of international tribunals is to strike a balance between these concerns in the interpretation of IIA provisions. Whether existing decisions have done this appropriately is a source of controversy among various interested parties. Certain trends of reasoning can be discerned on major issues. Accordingly, this part of the paper will identify those trends and consider their impact on the rights and obligations of investors and host countries in the light of development concerns.

1.   Right of establishment

The issue of admission refers to the entry of investments and investors of a contracting party into the territory of another contracting party. According to customary international law, countries have the right to regulate or prohibit the admission of foreign investors – and consequently, of their investments – into their territories. Traditionally, most countries have refrained from granting foreign nationals and companies an unrestricted right to invest in their economies. Most IIAs protect only investment that has been admitted into, and established in, the territory of the host country in accordance with the latter's domestic legislation (UNCTAD 1999a). To date, apart from United States and Canadian BITs, few such agreements grant rights of establishment, although this is becoming a more common element in other IIAs, notably in bilateral and regional free trade agreements with investment provisions (UNCTAD 2007; 2006a).

Pre-establishment rights granted in IIAs extend certain treaty protections – in particular, most-favoured-nation (MFN) treatment and national treatment – to the stage at which an investor is making its investment in the host country.[137] These IIAs have been designed with the purpose of ensuring the free entry of foreign investments – albeit with country-specific reservations – into the territory of the host country. Usually, a host country will regard foreign investment in certain sectors of its economy as contrary to its domestic legislation or to its vital national interests. Thus, when a right of establishment appears in an IIA, the parties retain some degree of flexibility to control the admission of FDI from the other party, usually by allowing for the inclusion of a list of industries, activities or laws and regulations that may be exempted from the obligations to grant national treatment and MFN treatment to the pre-establishment phase of the investment.

Following this pattern, the NAFTA and NAFTA-type agreements, such as the Japan–Singapore FTA, provide for the application of national treatment to the pre-establishment phase subject to country-specific exceptions.[138] Such exceptions may permit the exclusion of certain sectors and industries from pre-establishment obligations. This "negative list" approach to exceptions can be contrasted with a "positive list" approach, such as that adopted under the market access provisions of the General Agreement on Trade in Services (GATS), which extend pre-establishment protection only to sectors or industries specifically included in the schedule of commitments of a GATS contracting party. Thus, IIA provisions set limits to the extent of liberalization and protection that they provide with regard to pre-establishment issues. An example is the Canadian model Foreign Investment Promotion and Protection Agreement, which excludes from dispute settlement a decision by the Canadian authorities as regards an acquisition of a domestic company.

Most IIAs, in particular BITs, do not include pre-establishment rights. Thus, it is not surprising that there has not been much ISDS jurisprudence addressing this subject. To the extent that it exists, it is basically limited to one issue – that is, whether pre-investment expenditures undertaken by a potential investor qualify to be an "*investment*". This has been one of the central questions that arbitral tribunals have addressed in the three most relevant cases on this matter, namely *Mihaly International Corporation v. Sri Lanka*,[139] *Zhinvali Development Limited v. Georgia*[140] and *William Nagel v. Czech Republic*.[141]

Mihaly was the first occasion when an arbitral tribunal had been asked to determine the status of pre-investment expenditures under the ICSID Convention or under an IIA.[142] The question is relevant since under Article 25(1) of the ICSID Convention the jurisdiction of arbitral tribunals is limited to "*any legal dispute arising directly out of an investment* [...]". Thus, if a dispute arises because of measures undertaken before the investment was made, it is questionable whether it falls within the jurisdiction of ICSID.

Mihaly concerned the pre-establishment expenditures incurred with a proposed BOT (build, own, transfer) thermal power station project in Sri Lanka. Out of the 25 groups that had originally expressed interest, five were invited to enter into negotiations, one of which – Mihaly International Corporation – an enterprise incorporated in California, was selected.

Mihaly and Sri Lanka negotiated for several months, but in vain, to conclude a definitive agreement. Although no formal contract was ever signed between the parties, the Government of Sri Lanka issued a letter of intent during the negotiations, as well as a letter of agreement and a letter of extension. The letter of intent described the framework for the negotiations that would lead to the BOT agreement. It was specified that that document constituted only a declaration of intention, and did not establish binding obligations on either party.

After the issuance of the letter of intent, Mihaly incurred significant expenditures in negotiating project documents and trying to arrange financing, among other things. Mihaly sought to obtain reimbursement of its expenditures plus lost profits in the abandoned project.

Mihaly argued that its development activities were essential for the successful operation of the BOT project, including the physical construction of a plant, and that it was standard business practice to include pre-investment expenditures in the investment. Further, it argued that in the absence of a precise definition of the term "investment" in the applicable IIA or the ICSID Convention, it should be given a broad meaning in order to encourage a freer flow of capital into developing countries.

Sri Lanka argued that Mihaly's claim should be rejected, and described it as a "*claim [...] for reimbursement of expenditures made pursuing a possible investment in a proposed power project in Sri Lanka that never happened*".[143] Furthermore, it argued that developing countries would find it difficult to adhere to the ICSID Convention if, by means of a broad interpretation, a tribunal was to hold that the expenditures incurred in the present case could be characterized as "investments" in the absence of explicit State consent.

Mihaly did not refer to the fact that the BIT between Sri Lanka and the United States (1991) is not limited to admitted investment, and that the definition of "investment" included therein, much as in the majority of IIAs, is broad, explicitly covering assets such as "*claims to money or a claim to performance having an economic value, and associated with an investment*", or "*rights conferred by law or contract, and any licenses and permits pursuant to law*".[144]

The tribunal concluded as follows:

"*[...] The Claimant has not succeeded in furnishing any evidence of treaty interpretation or practice of States, let alone that of developing countries or Sri Lanka for that matter, to the effect that pre-investment and development expenditures in the circumstances of the present case could automatically be admitted as "investment" in the absence of the consent of the host State to the implementation of the project. It should be observed that while the US-Sri Lanka BIT contains provisions regarding the definition of investment and conditions for its admission, they recognize the Parties' prerogative in this respect. The Tribunal is consequently unable to accept as a valid denomination of "investment", the unilateral or internal characterization of certain expenditures by the Claimant in preparation for a project of investment. [...]*"[145]

It should be noted that although the tribunal held that the claimant had failed to show that the pre-investment expenditures amounted to an "investment", it did not reject the possibility that a pre-investment expenditure could constitute a protected investment under the ICSID Convention in two different situations. One would be where there is an agreement between the parties to regard pre-investment as protected investment under the ICSID Convention. Alternatively, if the State and the foreign investor reached a final agreement in order to materialize an investment, pre-investment expenditures might well be included in the category of investment, at least in terms of qualification for damages in the event of their loss or frustration once the investment had materialized.[146]

After the dispute in *Mihaly v. Sri Lanka*, two other arbitration tribunals addressed the issue of pre-investment expenditures, namely *Zhinvali Development Limited v. Georgia*[147] and *William Nagel v. Czech Republic*.[148]

The *Zhinvali* case concerned a dispute in connection with the proposed rehabilitation of a hydroelectric power plant in Georgia. For three years, Zhinvali Development Limited, an enterprise incorporated in Ireland, negotiated with the Government of Georgia; however, after pressure from international financial institutions to maintain a competitive and transparent bidding process for the project, no agreement was reached and Zhinvali was excluded from the project. The company then submitted a claim to ICSID for the reimbursement of expenses arising from feasibility studies, consultancy costs, travel expenses, legal fees and lost profits on the failed project.

In this case, the tribunal examined whether under the 1996 Georgia Investment Law and under Article 25(1) of the ICISD Convention the development costs qualified as "investments". As Georgia's express or implicit consent to the treatment of the claimant's development costs as an "investment" could not be demonstrated, the tribunal concluded that Zhinvali's expenditures did not fall within the limits of the 1996 Investment Law, and, as a result, those development costs could not be considered as an "investment" within the meaning of Article 25(1) of the ICSID Convention.[149]

In *William Nagel v. Czech Republic* the dispute involved a cooperation agreement negotiated between Mr. Nagel, a British national, and a State telecommunications company (Sra) wholly owned by the Czech Republic. In accordance with the agreement, the parties established a consortium and sought to obtain the necessary licences and permits to establish and operate a mobile telephone network in the Czech Republic. The Czech authorities held a public tender for two mobile telephone contracts, neither of which was awarded to Mr. Nagel. Thus, the latter submitted a claim to the Stockholm Chamber of Commerce on the basis of the BIT between the United Kingdom and the Czech Republic (1990), and argued that the Czech Government had deprived him of the rights that he had acquired through the cooperation agreement signed with the State telecommunications company. Mr. Nagel argued that his rights under the cooperation agreement constituted "*claims to money or to any performance under contract having a financial value*", and thus fell within the definition of "investment" used in the BIT.

The tribunal considered that "*financial value*" was an intrinsic element of the BIT's concept of investment, which had to fulfill two requirements: first, the value had to be real, and not just potential, and second, the concept of financial value had to be interpreted in connection with domestic law, since the latter determined to a great extent whether something had a financial value. Further, the tribunal found that the cooperation agreement was signed between Mr. Nagel and Sra, a State company; it did not find any convincing evidence of any concrete involvement of the Czech Government in the conclusion of that agreement. After examining the legal significance of the cooperation agreement under Czech law, the tribunal found that the rights derived therefrom did not have a financial value, and consequently did not constitute an asset or an investment protected under the BIT.

In sum, ISDS jurisprudence on pre-investment expenditures is limited; it is thus difficult to determine whether the findings in *Mihaly*, *Zhinvali* and *Nagel* have established a pattern in ISDS practice, except insofar as there has been a reluctance in all of the findings to consider pre-investment expenditures as protected investments under the ICSID Convention. Furthermore, as explained above (in subsection II.B), regardless of the agreement of the parties involved, recent ISDS jurisprudence has confirmed the view that, for the purposes of the ICSID Convention, the term "investment" is an objective precondition for jurisdiction. Furthermore, for an asset to be considered an "investment", several criteria identified by ISDS jurisprudence have to be met.

2. Fair and equitable treatment, and full protection and security

IIAs usually include one or several general principles that, together or individually, are intended to provide overall criteria by which to judge whether the treatment accorded to an investment is satisfactory.[150] Fair and equitable treatment is one of those general principles. It originated in customary international law on the protection of the property of aliens, and provides a basic standard, detached from the host country's domestic law, against which the behaviour of the host country vis-à-vis foreign investments can be assessed.

Numerous investment instruments combine the fair and equitable treatment standard with other legal principles that may have their own specific content and historical origin, such as the principles of "full protection and security"[151] and "non-discrimination".[152] While some agreements guarantee only fair and equitable treatment, other IIAs combine the three standards — or sometimes only two of them — into one single article.

Contrary to other treaty obligations, the fair and equitable treatment standard lacks a precise meaning. Consequently, it has raised important questions in international investment law, originally in the context of the application of NAFTA's Chapter 11, but more recently also in the context of several BIT-related investment disputes. The discussion has focused on the nature and content of the commitment. In this regard, two schools of thought have emerged in international legal doctrine.

According to some scholars, the obligation to grant "fair and equitable treatment" requires no more than the international minimum standard, which forms part of customary international law. In the view of other scholars, however, "fair and equitable treatment" means something different than the international minimum standard. They believe that the term should be given its plain ordinary meaning.[153] This results in applying a test based on equity on a case-by-case basis in order to determine whether the standard has been infringed.

Potential controversies about the content of the standard can be minimized depending on the specific language used in the IIA. Some IIAs contain more precise texts than others; thus, the amount of room for different interpretations of the fair and equitable treatment standard may vary significantly among different agreements.

a. ISDS experience under NAFTA

During the last decade, the determination of the scope and content of the fair and equitable treatment standard became a controversial issue in the context of NAFTA's Chapter 11 arbitrations, where arbitral tribunals were called on in several cases to interpret NAFTA's Article 1105 (1).[154] The debate was triggered by certain findings of the arbitration tribunals in three disputes, *Metalclad v. Mexico*,[155] *S.D.Myers v. Canada*[156] and *Pope & Talbot v. Canada*.[157]

In *Metalclad*, the tribunal determined that Mexico had not granted the investor fair and equitable treatment in accordance with international law because it had not acted in a manner consistent with the transparency obligations in NAFTA.[158] The award was finally set aside in part by the Supreme Court of British Columbia, which found that the tribunal had exceeded its jurisdiction by referring to conventional obligations included in treaties, which were beyond the scope of application of NAFTA's Chapter 11. According to the Court, the tribunal had not only interpreted Article 1105(1) of NAFTA in an extremely broad manner, but also failed to demonstrate that the principle of transparency, which was at stake in the case, had been incorporated into customary international law.[159] Thus, the Court asserted that the reference to "international law" in Article 1105 was to customary international law, and not to other conventional law.

In *S.D. Myers*, the tribunal found a violation of Article 1105(1) on the ground that the national treatment obligation under Article 1102 had been violated. It considered that the violation of a norm of international law that had been designed to protect foreign investors would be tantamount to a violation of Article 1105.[160]

In *Pope & Talbot*, after a long interpretative analysis of the terms "*fair and equitable treatment*" and "*full protection and security*" and their relationship with the international minimum standard, the tribunal concluded that those concepts entailed a treatment beyond that required under international law. Although the tribunal acknowledged that the text of Article 1105 suggested that "fair and equitable treatment" and "full protection and security" were elements which were included in the requirements of international law, it opted to deviate from the plain reading of the text and stated that there was another "possible interpretation" of that provision:

"*Another possible interpretation of the presence of fairness elements in Article 1105 is that they are additive to the requirements of international law. That is, investors under NAFTA are entitled to the international law minimum, plus the fairness elements. It is true that the language of Article 1105 suggests otherwise, since it states that the fairness elements are included in international law* [...]"[161]

The controversy generated by these three cases prompted the intervention of the NAFTA Free Trade Commission. On 31 July 2001, that Commission, comprising the Trade Ministers of the three signatory countries, issued a Note of Interpretation clarifying three basic points regarding NAFTA's Article 1105. First, it was stated that the provision prescribed the customary international law minimum standard of treatment of aliens as the minimum standard of treatment to be afforded to investments of investors of another party. Second, the Commission spelled out that the concepts of "*fair and equitable treatment*" and "*full protection and security*" do not require treatment in addition to, or beyond that, which is required by the customary international law minimum standard of treatment of aliens. Finally, the Commission concluded that the finding of a breach of another provision of the NAFTA, or of a separate international agreement, does not establish a violation of Article 1105(1).[162]

After this interpretation by the Free Trade Commission, several arbitral tribunals under NAFTA had to interpret Article 1105. Most tribunals have taken note of the Commission's guidance, and have recognized that they do not have unlimited discretion to decide when the standard has been breached, and that they rather have to base their assessment on the relevant sources of international law.[163] Nonetheless, ISDS jurisprudence regarding fair and equitable treatment in the NAFTA context has evolved on the basis of two important elements, which tribunals have consistently followed since 2002. First, it is recognized that the fair and equitable treatment standard has significantly evolved since *Neer* in the 1920s. Second, a breach of this "modern" fair and equitable treatment standard does not require that a State or agency of a State act in bad faith.

For example, in *Mondev International Inc v. United States*[164] – a dispute concerning property transactions in Boston between a Canadian developer and the city of Boston – the tribunal stated as follows:

"*Neer and like arbitral awards were decided in the 1920s, when the status of the individual in international law, and the international protection of foreign investments, were far less developed than they have since come to be. In particular, both the substantive and procedural rights of the individual in international law have undergone considerable development. In the light of these developments it is unconvincing to confine the meaning of "fair and equitable treatment" and "full protection and security" of foreign investments to what those terms – had they been current at the time – might have meant in the 1920s when applied to the physical security of an alien. To the modern eye, what is unfair or inequitable need not equate with the outrageous or the egregious. In particular, a State may treat foreign investment unfairly and inequitably without necessarily acting in bad faith. [...] the terms "fair and equitable treatment" and "full protection and security" had their origin in bilateral treaties in the post-war period. In these circumstances the content of the minimum standard today cannot be limited to the content of customary international law as recognised in arbitral decisions in the 1920s. [...] In holding that Article 1105(1) refers to customary international law, the FTC interpretations incorporate current international law, whose content is shaped by the conclusion of more than two thousand bilateral investment treaties and many treaties of friendship and commerce. Those treaties largely and concordantly provide for "fair and equitable" treatment of, and for "full protection and security" for, the foreign investor and his investments.*"[165] (emphasis added)

Thus, recent NAFTA arbitral tribunals have found that the customary international law to be applied is the customary international law as it stood in 1994 – and not in the 1920s at the time of *Neer*. The same view was held by the tribunals in *ADF Group v. United States*,[166] and in *Loewen Group, Inc. and Raymond*

Loewen v. United States.[167] In the latter dispute, the arbitral tribunal emphasized that bad faith was not required in order to breach the standard: "[n]*either State practice, the decisions of international tribunals nor the opinion or commentators support the view that bad faith or malicious intention is an essential element of unfair and inequitable treatment or denial of justice amounting to a breach of international justice"*.[168]

Subsequent tribunals have provided greater guidance about how to assess whether the standard has been violated in particular situations. These tribunals have required a certain degree of arbitrariness for the standard to be violated. For instance, in *Waste Management Inc. v. Mexico*[169] the tribunal reached the conclusion:

> "[...] *that the minimum standard of treatment of fair and equitable treatment is infringed by conduct attributable to the State and harmful to the claimant if the conduct is arbitrary, grossly unfair, unjust or idiosyncratic, is discriminatory and exposes the claimant to sectional or racial prejudice, or involves a lack of due process leading to an outcome which offends judicial propriety – as might be the case with a manifest failure of natural justice in judicial proceedings or a complete lack of transparency and candour in an administrative process. In applying this standard it is relevant that the treatment is in breach of representations made by the host State which were reasonably relied on by the claimant. [...] Evidently the standard is to some extent a flexible one which must be adapted to the circumstances of each case."*[170]

Furthermore, in *GAMI Investments Inc. v. Mexico*[171] – a dispute involving the implementation of the sugar regime in Mexico – the arbitral tribunal found that "[a] *claim of maladministration would likely violate Article 1105 if it amounted to an "outright and unjustified repudiation" of the relevant regulations"*. In *Methanex Corp. v. United States* the arbitral tribunal distinguished between the fair and equitable treatment standard as an absolute standard of protection and the relative standards of treatment included in NAFTA's Chapter 11, such as national treatment or MFN treatment. In this regard, the tribunal found that "[...] *the plain and natural meaning of the text of Article 1105 does not support the contention that the "minimum standard of treatment" precludes governmental differentiation as between nationals and aliens.*"[172]

b. *ISDS experience under other IIAs*

The wording in most IIAs is different from that of Article 1105. There are many types of fair and equitable treatment clauses. While some grant investments "*fair and equitable treatment*" and "*full protection and security*" in accordance with, or no less than provided under, international law,[173] other IIAs provide only for "*fair and equitable treatment*"[174] without making any reference to international law or to any other criteria to determine the content of the standard.

It should therefore not be surprising that ISDS experience regarding the application of the "*fair and equitable treatment*" standard in IIAs has not been entirely consistent over the last decade. On the basis of the scope given to the standard and the analytical approach used to determine its content, the arbitral decisions regarding this particular subject can be broadly classified into three categories.

Into the first category fall decisions that tend to follow a semantic approach, leading to a broad scope of application of the standard. These decisions do not make any reference to customary international law in order to determine whether the standard has been respected. The decisions in *Emilio Agustín Maffezini v. Spain* and *Middle East Cement Shipping and Handling Co. S.A. v. Egypt* are examples of this first category. In *Maffezini*, the tribunal dealt with the issue in the context of a transfer by a government official of funds from a private bank account in Spain. The tribunal found that "[...] *the lack of transparency with which this loan transaction was conducted is incompatible with Spain's commitment to ensure the investor a fair and equitable treatment in accordance with Article 4(1) of the [...] treaty* [between Argentina and Spain]".[175]

In *Middle East Cement* the tribunal considered that the failure to give full formal notice directly to a shipowner regarding the impending seizure of a ship despite the fact that such notice was placed on the ship itself was at variance with the requirements of the fair and equitable treatment standard in the BIT between Egypt and Greece (1993). The tribunal stated as follows:

> "[...] *Art. 2.2 of the BIT requires that "Investments by investors of a Contracting Party shall, at all times, be accorded fair and equitable treatment and shall enjoy full protection and security, in the territory of the other Contracting Party." This BIT provision must be given particular relevance in view of the special protection granted by Art. 4 against measures "tantamount to expropriation," and in the requirement for "due process of law" in Art.4.a). Therefore, a matter as important as the seizure and auctioning of a ship of the Claimant should have been notified by a direct communication for which the law No. 308 provided under the 1st paragraph of Art. 7, irrespective of whether there was a legal duty or practice to do so by registered mail with return receipt requested as argued by Claimant. The Tribunal finds that the procedure in fact applied here does not fulfill the requirements of Art. 2.2 and 4 of the BIT.*"[176] (emphasis added)

The second category of arbitral decisions tended to favour a more restricted approach when applying the standard, following the reasoning *Neer* and linking the standard to customary international law. An illustration of this approach is the arbitral decision in *Alex Genin, Eastern Credit Limited, Inc. v. Estonia*.[177] That dispute, which concerned the revocation of a banking licence granted to an investor, was submitted under the BIT between the United States and Estonia (1994).[178]

The tribunal found that despite the fact that certain procedures followed by the Estonian authorities did not conform with Estonian law and could be characterized as being contrary to generally accepted banking and regulatory practices, those procedures did not constitute a breach of the standard because there were ample grounds for the action taken by the Bank of Estonia:

> "*Article II(3)(a) of the BIT requires the signatory governments to treat foreign investment in a "fair and equitable" way. Under international law, this requirement is generally understood to "provide a basic and general standard which is detached from the host State's domestic law." While the exact content of this standard is not clear, the Tribunal understands it to require an "international minimum standard" that is separate from domestic law, but that is, indeed, a minimum standard. Acts that would violate this minimum standard would include acts showing a willful neglect of duty, an insufficiency of action falling far below international standards, or even subjective bad faith. Under the present circumstances – where ample grounds existed for the action taken by the Bank of Estonia – Respondent cannot be held to have violated Article II(3)(a) of the BIT.*"

In this case, the tribunal did not engage in a textual analysis of the clause in the BIT between Estonia and the United States. Instead, it referred to how this requirement had been generally understood under international law.

The third category of arbitral decisions links the fair and equitable treatment standard to customary international law, but at the same time notes that customary international law has evolved since the *Neer* case. Thus, as in the case of NAFTA tribunals, these decisions hold that to "[...] *the modern eye, what is unfair or inequitable need not to equate with the outrageous or the egregious. In particular, a State may treat foreign investment unfairly and inequitably without necessarily acting in bad faith.*"[179]

Furthermore, this group of decisions, which comprises recent awards in cases such as *CMS Gas Transportation Company v. Argentina*[180] and *Azurix Corp. v. Argentina*, tend to consider that there is a growing convergence between the plain meaning approach and the evolving content of customary international law. In this regard, the tribunal in *Azurix* stated as follows:

"The question whether fair and equitable treatment is or is not additional to the minimum treatment requirement under international law is a question about the substantive content of fair and equitable treatment and, whichever side of the argument one takes, the answer to the question may in substance be the same."[181]

Furthermore, an important element in the analysis that was introduced in *Tecnicas Medioambientales Tecmed S.A. v. Mexico*[182] and other recent BIT-based decisions is the general expectations of the foreign investor when making the investment.

The *Tecmed* dispute concerned the denial of a licence renewal for the operation of a hazardous waste landfill. Tecmed, a company incorporated in Spain, submitted the claim invoking the BIT between Mexico and Spain (1995), whose Article 4(1) provided that "[e]*ach Contracting Party will guarantee in its territory fair and equitable treatment, according to International Law, for the investments made by investors of the other Contracting Party*". The *Tecmed* tribunal interpreted this provision in the following manner:

*"The Arbitral Tribunal finds that the commitment of fair and equitable treatment included in Article 4(1) of the Agreement is an expression and part of the bona fide principle recognized in international law, although bad faith from the State is not required for its violation. […] The Tribunal considers that this provision of the Agreement, in light of the good faith principle established by international law, requires the Contracting Parties to provide to international investments treatment that **does not affect the basic expectations that were taken into account by the foreign investor to make the investment**. The foreign investor expects the host State to act in a consistent manner, free from ambiguity and totally transparently in its relations with the foreign investor, so that it may know before hand any and all rules and regulations that will govern its investments. […] **Therefore, compliance by the host State with such pattern of conduct is closely related to the above-mentioned principle, to the actual chances of enforcing such principle, and to excluding the possibility that state action be characterized as arbitrary, i.e. as presenting insufficiencies that would be recognized "**[…] **by any reasonable and impartial man", or although not in violation of specific regulations, as being contrary to the law because: [...] (it) shocks, or at least surprises, a sense of juridical propriety.*"[183] (emphasis added)

The merging of the textual interpretation with the notions of investor expectations and evolving international law is also evident in the *CMS* award. Referring to the experience of investors in the recent Argentine financial crisis, and its relation to the fair and equitable standard provided in the applicable BIT, the tribunal stated as follows:

"273. The key issue the Tribunal has to decide is whether the measures adopted [by Argentina] *in 2000-2002 breached the standard of protection afforded by Argentina's undertaking to provide fair and equitable treatment. The Treaty, like most bilateral investment treaties, does not define the standard of fair and equitable treatment and to this extent Argentina's concern about it being somewhat vague is not entirely without merit.*

274. The Treaty Preamble makes it clear, however, that one principal objective of the protection envisaged is that fair and equitable treatment is desirable "to maintain a stable framework for investments and maximum effective use of economic resources". There can be no doubt, therefore, that a stable legal and business environment is an essential element of fair and equitable treatment.

275. The measures that are complained of did in fact entirely transform and alter the legal and business environment under which the investment was decided and made. The discussion above, about the tariff regime and its relationship with a dollar standard and adjustment mechanism unequivocally shows that these elements are no longer present in the regime governing the business operations of the Claimant. It has also been established that the guarantees given in this connection under the legal framework and its various components were crucial for the investment decision.

276. In addition to the specific terms of the Treaty, the significant number of treaties, both bilateral and multilateral, that have dealt with this standard also unequivocally shows that fair and equitable treatment is inseparable from stability and predictability. Many arbitral decisions and scholarly writings point in the same direction.

277. It is not a question of whether the legal framework might need to be frozen as it can always evolve and be adapted to changing circumstances, but neither is it a question of whether the framework can be dispensed with altogether when specific commitments to the contrary have been made. The law of foreign investment and its protection has been developed with the specific objective of avoiding such adverse legal effects."[184]

In sum, the overall result of the arbitral decisions to date is that the fair and equitable treatment standard no longer prohibits solely egregious abuses of government power, or disguised uses of government powers for untoward purposes, but any open and deliberate use of government powers that fails to meet the requirements of good governance, such as transparency, protection of the investor's legitimate expectations, freedom from coercion and harassment, due process and procedural propriety, and good faith. In addition, in order to determine whether there has been compliance with the standard, it is relevant to consider whether the treatment is in breach of representations made by the host country that were reasonably relied upon by the investor.[185]

This may create compliance problems particularly in countries with less developed regulatory and administrative processes. On the other hand, the awards cited above also take into account the actual circumstances under which the foreign investor operates.[186] This includes, for instance, factors such as the familiarity of the investor with the host country and its economic, administrative and procedural practices, the degree of speculative risk freely undertaken by the investor, and the extent of his compliance with legal requirements.

c. Additional aspects regarding the standard of full protection and security

The standard of *full protection and security* has traditionally applied to foreign investors in periods of insurrection, civil unrest and other public disturbances, although it is not explicitly limited to those circumstances. ISDS jurisprudence has traditionally held that the full protection and security standard encompasses damage or losses sustained by an investor as a result of such violent episodes, whether directly due to government acts or to a lack of adequate protection of the investment by government officials or police.

Tribunals have indicated that the obligation is not one of result – that is, it is not a complete insurance policy against any and every loss due to some form of civil strife. However, the standard of care required has been set at a fairly high level. For example, comparisons with treatment of domestic nationals in cases of similar strife have been rejected. Arguments of incapacity or higher priorities in responding to the circumstances of the strife have also been dismissed as a basis for a defense to a claim. In essence, while not an obligation of result, recent cases have established an obligation of good faith efforts to protect the foreign-owned property, without special regard to the resources available to do so.[187] This has been referred to as a standard of "due diligence" on the part of the host country. As a result, this standard should be understood as being very much a "living" one, placing a clear premium on political stability.

Traditionally, the standard of full protection and security has been identified as part of the minimum standard of treatment (UNCTAD 1999c); nevertheless, it has remained a clear and distinct standard with a precise content – the "due diligence" duty mentioned above. At least three ICSID cases have focused on this particular obligation in recent years.[188] While this standard has been primarily used in situations of violence, there have been some recent examples of its application in non-violent situations in the sense of providing legal protection and security.[189]

The application of the full protection and security standard in non-violent contexts risks merging this specific standard with the more general standard of fair and equitable treatment. This development can be observed in some recent arbitral decisions. Some tribunals have found that the full protection and security standard has been breached because the investment has been subject to unfair and inequitable treatment.

For instance, in *Occidental Exploration and Production Company v. Ecuador,*[190] the standard was found to have been breached despite the non-existence of any physical violence or damage. The dispute in *Occidental* stemmed from the execution of a contract between a United States company and Petroecuador, an Ecuadorian State company in charge of the exploration and production of oil in Ecuador. After finding that Ecuador – by revoking previous decisions regarding the contract – had frustrated the legitimate expectations of the investor when the investment was made, the tribunal found as follows:

> "*The Tribunal accordingly holds that the Respondent has breached its obligations to accord fair and equitable treatment under Article II(3)(a) of the Treaty. In the context of this finding the question of whether in addition there has been a breach of full protection and security under this Article becomes moot as treatment that is not fair and equitable automatically entails an absence of full protection and security of the investment.*"[191]

The merging of the standard of full protection and security with the fair and equitable treatment standard in *Occidental* seems odd, especially when account is taken of the fact that the applicable IIA – the 1993 BIT between Ecuador and the United States – provided for both standards separately. Article II.2(a) of that BIT stipulates that "*Investment shall at all times be accorded fair and equitable treatment, shall enjoy full protection and security* [...]". Furthermore, the tribunal did not furnish any explanation for not paying attention to the specific wording of the BIT. The approach used in *Occidental* has been followed by other arbitral tribunals. In the recent decision in *Azurix v. Argentina,*[192] the tribunal repeated the reasoning in *Occidental*, and merged the full protection and security standard with the fair and equitable treatment principle. Noting that the applicable provision was identical with the article in the BIT between Ecuador and the United States, the tribunal stated as follows:

> "*The Tribunal is persuaded of the interrelationship of fair and equitable treatment and the obligation to afford the investor full protection and security. [...] full protection and security was understood to go beyond protection and security ensured by the police. It is not only a matter of physical security; the stability afforded by a secure investment environment is as important from an investor's point of view. The Tribunal is aware that in recent free trade agreements signed by the United States, for instance, with Uruguay, full protection and security is understood to be limited to the level of police protection required under customary international law. However, when the terms "protection and security" are qualified by "full" and no other adjective or explanation, they extend, in their ordinary meaning, the content of this standard beyond physical security. To conclude, the Tribunal, having held that the Respondent failed to provide fair and equitable treatment to the investment, finds that the Respondent also breached the standard of full protection and security under the BIT.*"[193]

It may be too early to tell whether the findings in *Occidental* and *Azurix* will establish a new pattern in ISDS practice.

3. National treatment

The wording of the national treatment provisions varies considerably from one IIA to another. Some IIAs provide a national treatment guarantee to the investors as well as to the investments, others only to the investments, and some – albeit a smaller number than the others – refrain from granting this standard at all (UNCTAD 1999b). Consequently, ISDS practice on this particular subject cannot be generalized with regard to all IIAs. However, regardless of the particular wording used in investment agreements, national treatment is a non-contingent standard in all cases, the content of which has to be determined by reference to the treatment granted by the host country to its investors and their investments.

Some IIAs, as is the case of Article 1102 of NAFTA, explicitly state that the obligation to grant treatment no less favourable to the covered investments or investors should apply only when the latter are in "*like circumstances*" with domestic investments and investors.[194] In these situations, the interpretation of national treatment provisions also requires that there be a determination of which entities or activities serve as a reference point for ascertaining the type of treatment to be granted. Here, the concept of "like circumstances" becomes an important premise of the application of the national treatment standard.

Over the last decade, most of the ISDS practice regarding national treatment has developed in the context of the interpretation of Article 1102 of NAFTA. Most arbitral tribunals have followed a three-step analysis in order to determine whether in a particular case a host country has breached its obligation to provide national treatment to covered investors and their investments. Those three steps are as follows: identification of the relevant subjects for comparison; second, consideration of the relative treatment each comparator receives, and third, if a different treatment is found, examination of whether the subjects compared are in "like circumstances", or in other words, whether there are any factors that may justify differential treatment. ISDS experience regarding each of these steps is examined below.

a.   *Identification of the subjects for comparison*

Regarding the first step of the analysis, most arbitral tribunals have recognized from the outset, that national treatment is a relative, non-contingent standard. Hence its interpretation necessarily calls for a comparison to be made between the investor invoking its right and someone else. One of the issues that have frequently arisen in the context of investment disputes is the determination of who should be the other subject whose treatment will be compared with that received by the foreign investor.

In *Pope & Talbot v. Canada*[195] the dispute involved the imposition by Canada of an export-fee regime on the export of softwood lumber from its territory to the United States. That regime was implemented by Canada in order to comply with an agreement negotiated with the United States in order to avoid the imposition of countervailing duties by the latter on lumber exported from Canada's four largest softwood-producing provinces. The regime was founded upon a complex formula based on historical export performance as a criterion for the entitlement to export lumber "fee free". The regime was applied only to softwood lumber producers from the four provinces targeted. A United States investor, Pope & Talbot, claimed that, among other things, that regime breached the national treatment standard.

In *Pope & Talbot* the tribunal stated that the comparison should generally be made between the foreign investor or its investment on the one hand, and any domestic investors or investments operating in the same business or economic sector on the other hand. The basis for such an approach was found in jurisprudence of the General Agreement on Tariffs and Trade (GATT) and international treaty sources, such as the 1976 Declaration on National Treatment for Foreign-Controlled Enterprises of the Organisation for Economic Co-operation and Development (OECD). In this regard, the *Pope & Talbot* tribunal stated:

> "*In evaluating the implications of the legal context, the Tribunal believes that, as a first step, the treatment accorded a foreign owned investment protected by Article 1102(2) should be compared with that accorded domestic investments in the same business or economic sector.*"[196]

Many other arbitral tribunals also used this approach, identifying the appropriate comparator on the basis of the effects that the challenged measure had on other investors or investments in the same business or economic sector. For instance, in *S.D. Myers v. Canada,* where the dispute involved a ban on exports of

PCB wastes to the United States which impeded S.D. Myers from undertaking its business of shipping PCB wastes from Canada to its Ohio facilities for treatment and destruction, the tribunal compared would-be competitors in the Canadian market for the destruction of PCB wastes.

In *Marvin Roy Feldman v. the United Mexican States*,[197] the dispute involved a trading company that imported, among other things, cigarettes from the United States for resale in Mexico. Feldman's company had qualified to receive tax rebates during certain periods of time, but not others. During these same periods, local competitors were still receiving rebates. Feldman's company was also subjected to much more rigorous audits than its competitors. In this case, the arbitrators stated that the group of comparable investors and investments was composed of those enterprises engaged in the purchase and resale of cigarettes.

However, to identify the particular domestic investors that are in the same business or economic sector as the foreign investor is not always an easy matter. One of the recent cases in which the question of the identification of the proper comparator was the key aspect of the dispute was *Methanex v. United States*.[198] The dispute involved a ban eliminating the use of MTBE, a gasoline additive, in California. Methanex, a Canadian company that produced methanol, a primary ingredient of MTBE, claimed that the California's ban breached, inter alia, the national treatment standard. The basis for that claim was that, in Methanex's view, the ban on MTBE had the effect of benefiting the United States producers of ethanol, a product that was a direct substitute for MTBE. The identification of which was the proper comparator was particularly relevant, as there were many producers of methanol in the United States that were affected in the same manner as Methanex by the ban on MTBE. In this dispute, the arbitral tribunal referred to *Pope & Talbot*, and stated as follows:

> "*In this respect, the NAFTA award in Pope & Talbot v. Canada is instructive. There, a US investor in Canada, which was obliged to pay export fees, alleged that it was in like circumstances with Canadian producers in other provinces that were not subject to export fees. The tribunal, however, rejected the claim for there were more than 500 Canadian producers in other provinces which were subject to the fees. That is, the tribunal selected the entities that were in the most "like circumstances" and not comparators that were in less "like circumstances". It would be a forced application of Article 1102 if a tribunal were to ignore the identical comparator and to try to lever in an, at best, approximate (and arguably inappropriate) comparator. The fact stands – Methanex did not receive less favourable treatment than the identical domestic comparators, producing methanol.*"

Thus, the award in *Methanex v. United States* clarified further the criteria for identifying the appropriate comparator in a national treatment analysis. In this regard, the tribunal basically stated that the foreign investor or foreign-owned investment should be compared with a domestic investor or domestically owned investment that was like it in all relevant aspects, except nationality of ownership. That assertion was based on the reasoning that it is necessary to compare the treatment of the foreign investor with the treatment accorded to a domestic investor whose situation is the most similar. Since the purpose of the national treatment standard is to address discrimination applied to an investment on the basis of nationality, "*in ideal circumstances, the foreign investor or foreign-owned investment should be compared to a domestic investor or domestically-owned investment that is like it in all relevant respects, but for nationality of ownership*".[199]

The *Methanex* tribunal thus took a narrow approach to the requirement "*in like circumstances*" by asking whether the activities of the foreign investor were comparable with economic activities in the domestic sphere, rather than the relatively broader approach used in *S.D. Myers,* and drawing upon the precedents in the area of international trade. Hence, there is currently no uniform interpretation of the "in like circumstances" requirement.

b. *Comparison of treatment of the foreign investor with that of the domestic investor*

Following the trend established by most arbitral tribunals over the last decade, the second step in a national treatment analysis consists in observing whether there are differences in treatment between the foreign investor and its domestic counterpart. Regarding this specific aspect, the arbitral tribunal in *S.D. Myers*, one of the first established under NAFTA's Chapter 11, made two important findings. First, it recognized that a breach of the national treatment standard could be de jure or de facto. Thus, the scope of the analysis is not limited to a de jure legal or administrative discrimination, but also comprises treatment that, despite not being discriminatory on its face, nevertheless has a discriminatory impact on the foreign investors or their investments. In this regard, the tribunal explicitly stated as follows:

> *"The Tribunal takes the view that, in assessing whether a measure is contrary to a national treatment norm, the following factors should be taken into account:*
> - *whether the practical effect of the measure is to create a disproportionate benefit for nationals over non nationals;*
> - *whether the measure, on its face, appears to favour its nationals over non-nationals who are protected by the relevant treaty.*
> *Each of these factors must be explored in the context of all the facts to determine whether there actually has been a denial of national treatment."*[200]

The recognition that the national treatment standard can be breached by measures leading to de facto discrimination has been consistent in ISDS jurisprudence.

The second important finding that from the outset was clearly recognized by arbitral tribunals constituted under NAFTA's Chapter 11 is that, in order to demonstrate a de facto discrimination, it is neither necessary nor sufficient to demonstrate any particular discriminatory intent on the part of the host country. In this regard, arbitral tribunals have held that:

> *"Intent is important, but protectionist intent is not necessarily decisive on its own. The existence of an intent to favour nationals over non-nationals would not give rise to a breach of Chapter 1102 of the NAFTA if the measure in question were to produce no adverse effect on the non-national complainant. The word "treatment" suggests that practical impact is required to produce a breach of Article 1102, not merely a motive or intent that is in violation of Chapter 11."*[201]

Furthermore, in *Feldman v. Mexico*, after stating that the national treatment standard is intended to protect against discrimination because of the foreign status of the investor, the tribunal also affirmed that there is no requirement to show that a breach of national treatment is expressly due to the investor's nationality. Rather, a de facto difference in treatment could stand on its own, *"at least in the absence of any evidence to the contrary"*.[202] Another reading of this case could be, however, that de facto discrimination violating national treatment exists only where it is based on the intent to discriminate on the basis of nationality. The tribunal essentially presumed intent to discriminate and put the burden on the State to disprove discriminatory intent.

c. *Whether foreign and domestic investors are in "like circumstances"*

In several IIAs, the obligation to grant to foreign investors and their investments a treatment no less favourable than that granted to domestic investors and their investments is conditional on the requirement that both investor or investment must be in "*like circumstances*".

In ISDS practice, the inclusion of the "*like circumstances*" element in national treatment provisions has had a legal impact similar to that of a treaty exception. That is, once the investor submitting the claim has demonstrated that it has received a treatment less favourable than that granted to domestic investors and their investments in the host country, it is up to the latter to demonstrate that the foreign investor is not less in "like circumstances" than its domestic competitors. Thus, once a difference in treatment has been found, it is left to the tribunal to determine whether investors or investments are in "like circumstances". Such a determination requires a factual analysis undertaken on a case-by-case basis.

It should be noted that the application of the national treatment standard in the context of IIAs entails dynamics that are different from those entailed by the application of the same standard in the context of international trade in goods. For a long time, a significant body of jurisprudence regarding the objective, nature and content of the national treatment standard has evolved in the context of the GATT and the World trade Organization (WTO) dispute settlement procedures. In numerous cases, this forum has considered allegations that a country has not treated foreign goods as favourably as "*like*" domestic goods. One of the main ways to address that question has been to determine whether the products produced by the domestic industry and those produced by foreign suppliers are in fact substitutes in the marketplace.[203]

In several cases in the context of NAFTA´s Chapter 11, arbitral tribunals have adopted an approach that provides host countries with significant scope for legitimate regulatory initiatives even if they treat domestic and foreign investors differently. In determining whether foreign and domestic investors that were treated differently were in like circumstances, arbitral tribunals have asked whether the difference in treatment has been justified by a rational policy objective that is not based on a preference for domestic over foreign investors and does not unduly undermine the investment liberalizing objectives of NAFTA. If the difference in treatment can be justified on this basis, arbitral tribunals have found that the foreign and domestic investors are not in like circumstances. For instance, in *Pope & Talbot*, the arbitral tribunal stated the following:

> "[...] *Differences in treatment will presumptively violate Article 1102(2), unless they have a reasonable nexus to rational government policies that (1) do not distinguish, on their face or de fact, between foreign-owned and domestic companies, and (2) do not otherwise unduly undermine the investment liberalizing objectives of NAFTA.*"[204]

In conclusion, the national treatment obligation remains open to further refinement given its interpretation by arbitral tribunals. The cases reviewed have accepted a standard of both de jure and de facto discrimination based on a case-by-case analysis of the impact that a measure has on a foreign investor. This allows for an examination not only of measures that clearly show difference of treatment between foreign and domestic investors that is favourable to the latter, but also of measures that are, on their face, non-discriminatory but have the effect of according less favourable treatment to foreign as compared with domestic investors in like circumstances.

4. Most-favoured-nation treatment

In addition to the national treatment standard, the other key non-discrimination obligation typically included in IIAs is MFN treatment. This principle entails that the host country will provide a covered foreign investor with the highest standard of treatment available to an investor from any other foreign country.

One of the most important lessons emerging from ISDS practice over the last decade is that the way in which MFN provisions are drafted in the various IIAs does matter, and that, depending on the wording of the applicable clause, a dispute can lead to different outcomes. The scope and approach used to draft MFN clauses in IIAs differ substantially among different agreements. Some IIAs provide that MFN applies to all matters covered by the treaty; others provide that MFN applies to all investments of investors, while yet others provide that MFN operates with respect to the management, maintenance, use, enjoyment and disposal of the investments. Other IIAs merge into one single provision the MFN and the fair and equitable treatment standard (UNCTAD 1999d). The variety of approaches used in IIAs to regulate the MFN obligation explains to a great extent why investment jurisprudence over the last decade has not been uniform on this subject.

One of the potential effects of the MFN standard is to broaden the scope of an investor's procedural and substantive rights beyond those in the original agreement under which he/she claims protection. This result has recently led to controversy based on the possibility of investors using the MFN clause to practice "treaty shopping", having the option to pick and choose provisions from the various IIAs signed by a host country. On the other hand, it could be argued that such an effect is precisely what MFN is all about, and that many public policy considerations could justify that result.

The interpretation of the MFN standard by international jurisprudence is not a recent development.[205] Most of the ISDS practice addressed the MFN standard with regard to substantive rights. However, more recent investment case law also deals with the question whether the MFN standard should apply to dispute settlement procedures.

a.   *MFN and dispute settlement procedures*

Although it was not the first time that the issue arose in the context of an investment dispute,[206] one of the most controversial cases of the last decade addressing the question of the applicability of MFN to dispute settlement procedures has been *Maffezini v. Spain.*[207] This case concerned a dispute arising out of the treatment that Spanish authorities allegedly accorded to Emilio Agustin Maffezini, an Argentine national who invested in an enterprise for the production and distribution of chemical products in Galicia, Spain. Mr. Maffezini invoked the BIT between Spain and Argentina and initiated an international arbitral procedure before ICSID. According to Article 10 of the BIT between Argentina and Spain, the possibility of settling the dispute through international arbitration existed only once domestic tribunals had failed to resolve the dispute on the merits after an 18-month period had elapsed. To overcome that hurdle, Mr. Maffezini argued that the MFN clause in Article 4 of the BIT between Argentina and Spain allowed him to invoke the dispute settlement provisions in the BIT between Chile and Spain, which entitled the investor to submit the dispute to ICSID arbitration without having to submit it first to domestic courts. The MFN clause in the BIT between Spain and Argentina reads as follows:

"Article 4
Treatment

[…]
*2. **In all matters subject to this Agreement,** this treatment shall be no less favourable than that extended by each Party to the investments made in its territory by investors of a third country.* […]" (unofficial translation from Spanish, emphasis added)

Given that the wording of the MFN clause cited above explicitly referred to "*all matters subject to this Agreement*", the tribunal found, after elaborate reasoning, that in this particular case Mr. Maffezini could "import" the dispute settlement provisions of the BIT between Chile and Spain and avoid the requirement to submit his dispute to Spanish courts prior to initiating a case under ICSID.

Aware of the potential effects of this expansive interpretation of the MFN provision, the arbitral tribunal introduced several caveats for the application of the MFN standard. First, it noted that the scope of the MFN treatment has to be based on the text of the applicable agreement. Second, the tribunal referred to the *ejusdem generis* principle, whereby a MFN clause can apply only to matters belonging to the same subject matter or the same category of subject to which the clause relates. For instance, an advantage granted between two contracting parties in the context of a financial agreement cannot automatically be "imported" into an IIA by a contracting party invoking the MFN clause. Third, the tribunal introduced the limitation that the MFN standard should not be used to override public policy considerations envisaged by the contracting parties as crucial for conditioning their acceptance of the agreement. In this regard, the arbitral tribunal stated as follows:

"*Notwithstanding the fact that the application of the most favoured nation clause to dispute settlement arrangements in the context of investment treaties might result in the harmonization and enlargement of the scope of such arrangements, there are some important limits that ought to be kept in mind. As a matter of principle, the beneficiary of the clause should not be able to override public policy considerations that the contracting parties might have envisaged as fundamental conditions for their acceptance of the agreement in question, particularly if the beneficiary is a private investor, as will often be the case. The scope of the clause might thus be narrower than it appears at first sight.*"[208]

Maffezini resulted in the highlighting of the importance of clearly delimiting the scope of application of the MFN clause in the text of these agreements. It made it clear to contracting parties that if they did not intend to extend MFN treatment to dispute settlement matters, it would be better for the IIA to explicitly say so.

The interpretation of the broad MFN provision in *Maffezini* influenced later arbitral tribunals, such as the one adjudicating in *Siemens v. Argentina*.[209] The discussion in *Siemens* was similar to that in *Maffezini*. In *Siemens*, the claimant sought to make a substantive claim against Argentina under the BIT negotiated between the latter and Germany (1991). That IIA, like the BIT between Spain and Argentina applicable in *Maffezini*, provided for an 18-month period in which Argentine courts had the opportunity to resolve the dispute. The claimant sought to avoid that provision by invoking the MFN principle and apply the BIT between Chile and Argentina (1991), which did not require a submission to local courts prior to arbitration. The MFN clause in the Argentina–Germany BIT states that none of the contracting parties shall accord in its territory to nationals or companies or their investments of the other contracting party "a less favourable treatment" than the treatment granted to nationals or companies or their investments of its own nationals or companies or to the investments of nationals or companies of third States. In Siemens, the tribunal concurred with the decision in *Maffezini*, and stated as follows:

"[…] *Access to these* [dispute settlement] *mechanisms is part of the protection offered under the Treaty. It is part of the treatment of foreign investors and investments and of the advantages accessible through a MFN clause.* […] *This conclusion concurs with the findings of the arbitral tribunal in Maffezini* [...]"[210]

The arbitral decisions in both *Maffezini* and *Siemens* generated some controversy among certain Governments, which did not consider that MFN should apply to dispute settlement procedures.[211] Furthermore, the interpretation of the MFN standard varied significantly in two successive investment disputes, in which arbitral tribunals took a more restrictive approach. The first of these cases was *Salini Costruttori S.p.A. and Italstrade S.p.A. v. Jordan*,[212] a dispute that entailed a claim by Italian investors under the BIT between Italy and Jordan (2001) based on the performance of a contract. The BIT explicitly stated that disputes arising from contracts had to be referred to the dispute settlement mechanisms provided for in the contracts. However, after finding that the dispute settlement provisions included in the BITs between Jordan and the United Kingdom (1979) and Jordan and the United States (1997) allowed investors to refer a contract-based claim to ICSID, the investors invoked the MFN clause of the BIT between Italy and Jordan in order to justify the submission of their claim to ICSID. Thus, the arbitral tribunal had to consider whether the MFN clause could be invoked for dispute settlement purposes.

The tribunal in *Salini v. Jordan* shared the concerns expressed in numerous quarters with regard to the solution adopted in *Maffezini*, and explicitly expressed its concern that despite the caveats entered by the tribunal in that dispute, such a broad interpretation of the MFN standard would add "*more uncertainties to the risk of "treaty shopping"* ". Thus, in *Salini v. Jordan*, the tribunal followed a more restrictive approach, and refrained from applying MFN to dispute settlement on the basis that the circumstances of that particular dispute were different. In this regard, the tribunal stated as follows:

"*The Tribunal observes that the circumstances of this case are different. Indeed, Article 3 of the BIT between Italy and Jordan does not include any provision extending its scope of* *application to dispute settlement. It does not envisage "all rights or all matters covered by the agreement." Furthermore, the Claimants have submitted nothing from which it <u>might</u> be established that the common intention of the Parties was to have the most-favored-nation clause apply to dispute settlement. Quite on the contrary, the intention as expressed in Article 9(2) of the BIT was to exclude from ICSID jurisdiction contractual disputes between an investor and an entity of a State Party in order that such disputes might be settled in accordance with the procedures set forth in the investment agreements. Lastly, the Claimants have not cited any practice in Jordan or Italy in support of their claims."*[213]

In 2005, the issue of the applicability of the MFN standard to dispute settlement procedures arose again, this time in *Plama Consortium Limited v. Bulgaria.*[214] This case concerned a dispute submitted under the BIT between Cyprus and Bulgaria (1987), which limited the application of ISDS procedures to disputes related to expropriation and did not envisage the possibility of submitting the dispute to ICSID. The MFN clause included in the BIT stated that each contracting party "[…] *shall apply to the investments in its territory by investors of the other Contracting Party a treatment which is not less favourable than that accorded to investments by investors of third states*". Thus, on the basis of the MFN provision, the claimant pretended to invoke the BIT between Bulgaria and Finland (1997), which included ISDS provisions applicable to all disputes related to investments. In this particular case, the arbitral tribunal addressed two main issues related to the MFN standard: whether the MFN provision in the BIT between Bulgaria and Cyprus applied to all aspects of "treatment"; and whether "treatment" covered settlement of dispute provisions in other BITs to which Bulgaria was a contracting party.

The tribunal concluded that the MFN provision could not be interpreted as providing consent to submission of a dispute under the BIT between Bulgaria and Cyprus to ICSID arbitration. Criticizing the approach used by the arbitral tribunal in *Maffezini* and in *Salini v. Jordan*, the tribunal based its reasoning on two fundamental premises. First, the arbitrators stressed that the main prerequisite for arbitration is an agreement of the parties to arbitrate. Consequently, it stated that:

"[…] *It is a well-established principle, both in domestic and international law, that such an agreement should be clear and unambiguous. In the framework of a BIT, the agreement to arbitrate is arrived at by the consent to arbitration that a state gives in advance in respect of investment disputes falling under the BIT, and the acceptance thereof by an investor if the latter so desires. […] Doubts as to the parties' clear and unambiguous intention can arise if the agreement to arbitrate is to be reached by incorporation by reference. [...]*"

The second basis for the tribunal's decision was the difficulty it found in applying an objective test to determine which dispute settlement procedure is more favourable. In this regard, the arbitrators stated as follows:

"*The Claimant argues that it is obviously more favorable for the investor to have a choice among different dispute resolution mechanisms, and to have the entire dispute resolved by arbitration as provided in the Bulgaria-Finland BIT, than to be confined to ad hoc arbitration limited to the quantum of compensation for expropriation. The Tribunal is inclined to agree with the Claimant that in this particular case, a choice is better than no choice. But what if one BIT provides for UNCITRAL arbitration and another provides for ICSID? Which is more favorable?*"

On the basis of those two premises, the tribunal in *Plama v. Bulgaria* concluded that it is not possible, through an MFN provision, to incorporate by reference dispute settlement provisions in whole or in part set forth in another treaty, "[…] *unless the MFN provision in the basic treaty leaves no doubt that the contracting parties intended to incorporate them*".

b.   MFN and substantive protection standards

The applicability of the standard to dispute settlement procedures is not the only MFN-related issue addressed by ISDS practice over the last decade. Other disputes have raised the question of whether broader or more comprehensive substantive protection provisions included in a given IIA can be invoked by an investor under an ISDS procedure established under a different IIA.

Regarding the application of the MFN standard, two main trends are evident in recent ISDS practice. First, as explained in the previous section, while investment jurisprudence interpreting national treatment has developed a sophisticated three-step approach to determine whether a particular measure breaches that obligation, ISDS practice with respect to MFN has not followed the same pattern. This may be due to the fact that jurisprudence on MFN has basically dealt with traditional BITs, which include MFN provisions simpler and more broadly drafted than those in NAFTA. Indeed, while the latter includes the qualifier that the MFN treatment provided to covered investors is provided in "*like circumstances*", numerous BITs simply make reference to the obligation of the host country to provide "MFN treatment".

Second, recent ISDS jurisprudence has not been particularly consistent regarding the ease with which substantive protection standards are "imported" into the context of a different IIA. Some arbitral tribunals have been cautious about automatically incorporating substantive protection provisions from other IIAs, and, following the limitations on the application of the MFN clause pointed out in *Maffezini*, have attempted to abstain from altering the underlying "bargain" implicit in the IIA which is the basis of the claim. However, following a totally opposite approach, other tribunals have easily applied substantive provisions from other IIAs to provide protection to a foreign investor invoking the MFN clause under a different investment agreement.

Among the tribunals following a cautious approach is the one in *Tecmed v. Mexico*. In the relevant part of its decision, this tribunal considered that matters relating to the application of an IIA involve the time dimension of application of its substantive provisions. Owing to their significance and importance, they go to the core of matters that must be specifically negotiated by the contracting parties. The *Tecmed* tribunal further stated:

> "[…] *These are determining factors for their acceptance of the Agreement, as they are directly linked to the identification of the substantive protection regime applicable to the foreign investor and, particularly, to the general (national or international) legal context within which such regime operates, as well as to the access of the foreign investor to the substantive provisions of such regime. **Their application cannot therefore be impaired by the principle contained in the most favored nation clause**.*"[215] (emphasis added)

The finding in *Tecmed v. Mexico* illustrates the trend whereby tribunals have recently limited the application of the MFN standard to situations where the additional rights "imported" from a different IIA do not impact on the balance of rights in a significant way, so as to "*go to the core of matters that must be specifically negotiated by the contracting parties*".[216]

As stated before, however, ISDS practice regarding MFN has not been consistent. A recent decision by an ICSID tribunal in *MTD Equity Bhd v. Chile*[217] illustrates a relatively liberal approach to the use of the MFN clause in an IIA. This dispute involved a Malaysian construction company that, after being authorized to invest in Chile, did not have its construction project approved because of zoning requirements. MTD submitted a claim under the Chile–Malaysia BIT (1992), and invoked the MFN clause in that IIA to "import" the provisions on fair and equitable treatment included in the BITs between Chile and Denmark (1993) and Chile and Croatia (1994). The tribunal considered whether the provisions of those two BITs, which include an obligation to award permits subsequent to approval of an investment, could be considered to be part of the fair and equitable treatment standard. The basis for framing the question in such a manner stems from the fact that Article 3.1 of the BIT between Chile and Malaysia merged the fair and equitable treatment standard with the MFN standard, and stated as follows:

"*Investments made by investors of either Contracting Party in the territory of the other Contracting Party shall receive treatment which is fair and equitable, and not less favourable than that accorded to investments made by investors of any third State.*"

On the basis of that provision, and without considering the limitations on the application of the MFN standard referred to by the arbitral tribunal in *Maffezini*, the tribunal in *MTD* simply concluded as follows:

"*The Tribunal has concluded that, under the BIT, the fair and equitable standard of treatment has to be interpreted in the manner most conducive to fulfill the objective of the BIT to protect investments and create conditions favorable to investments. The Tribunal considers that to include as part of the protections of the BIT those included in Article 3(1) of the Denmark BIT and Article 3(3) and (4) of the Croatia BIT is in consonance with this purpose. The Tribunal is further convinced of this conclusion by the fact that the exclusions in the MFN clause relate to tax treatment and regional cooperation, matters alien to the BIT but that, because of the general nature of the MFN clause, the Contracting Parties considered it prudent to exclude. A contrario sensu, other matters that can be construed to be part of the fair and equitable treatment of investors would be covered by the clause.*"[218]

Once more, *MTD* illustrates that the particular language used in the IIA provisions can have a practical impact, and lead to very different results from those originally envisaged by the contracting parties during negotiations.

5. Expropriation

Expropriation has traditionally ranked at the top of the controversial issues in the development of international law on investment. The international debate on expropriation for most of the twentieth century focused on the conditions under which an expropriation could be considered lawful. Today, it appears to be recognized that the basic principles of customary international law on expropriation state that foreign-owned property may not be expropriated, or subject to a measure tantamount to expropriation, unless four conditions are met: (1) the measure is for a public purpose; (2) it is taken in accordance with applicable laws and due process; (3) it is non-discriminatory; and (4) it is accompanied by compensation.[219]

This level of convergence regarding the requirements for a lawful expropriation having been reached, the debate has shifted over the last decade, and now focuses on the question of what amounts to an indirect expropriation of an investment. Most IIAs contain expropriation clauses which, despite protecting investment against unlawful "*expropriation*" or "*nationalization*" or "*measures having an equivalent effect*", do not define these terms or establish any factual criteria to determine whether a particular situation constitutes an expropriation. Thus, one of the aspects that has generated controversy in ISDS practice has been the lack of clarity of some IIAs regarding the degree of interference with the rights of ownership that is required for an act or a series of acts to constitute an indirect expropriation, with compensation thus being required.

International legal doctrine has traditionally distinguished between two broad categories of expropriation. First, there is the direct expropriation, which, as its name suggests, entails the actual taking of property by direct means, including the loss of all, or almost all, useful control over property. Second, there is the indirect taking, where the measure deprives the owner of the substantial benefits of the property, without formally expropriating him. One important kind of indirect taking is a regulatory expropriation, where a measure is taken for regulatory purposes, but has an impact on the economic value of the investment sufficient to be considered an expropriation (UNCTAD 2000).

The potential for investment disputes related to an alleged regulatory expropriation has significantly increased in recent years. In order to achieve its goals, the modern State needs regulation in a wide range of public policy areas. As the level of interaction between the State and the property rights of citizens increases, a main challenge is how to distinguish between a legitimate exercise of governmental authority and a regulatory taking that requires compensation (UNCTAD 2003, p. 111).

Numerous arbitral tribunals have addressed the issue of indirect expropriation over the last decade. However, the critical question as to which elements establish a taking under international law remains unsettled. The complexity of the issue explains why a unified methodology has so far failed to emerge from ISDS case law. Most arbitral tribunals that have addressed the question agree that the determination as to whether a regulatory taking has in fact occurred needs to be made on a case-by-case basis.

Despite the analytical difficulties referred to above, it is possible to identify various key elements repeatedly referred to by arbitral tribunals in the last decade in order to determine whether a country is liable to compensate an investor for an indirect taking. Among those elements are the permanence of the interference with the property, the substantiality of such interference, the existence of investment-backed expectations and, more recently, the proportionality between the public policy objective and the impact on the property rights of the investor.

Regarding the first element, ISDS practice has traditionally held that for an indirect expropriation to occur, the interference with the property of the investor must be permanent. Thus, for a taking to exist, tribunals have required a lasting deprivation of ownership rights. For instance, in *S.D. Myers*, when examining the export ban on PCB waste challenged by the claimant, the tribunal did not find that an indirect expropriation had happened because the export ban was temporary, ending after a 16-month period. In that dispute, the tribunal stated as follows:

> *"In this case, the Interim Order and the Final Order were designed to, and did, curb SDMI's initiative, but only for a time. Canada realized no benefit from the measure. The evidence does not support a transfer of property or benefit directly to others. An opportunity was delayed. The Tribunal concludes that this is not an "expropriation" case."*[220]

A second element consistently referred to by ISDS practice is the substantiality of the interference with the property rights. In this regard, arbitral tribunals have reiterated that not all government impediments to business operations amount to a taking and thus require compensation. For instance, in *Feldman v. Mexico*, the arbitral tribunal stated:

> *"[...] governments must be free to act in the broader public interest through the protection of the environment, new or modified tax regimes, the granting or withdrawal of government subsidies, reductions or increases in tariff levels, imposition of zoning restrictions and the like. Reasonable government regulation of this type cannot be achieved if any business that is adversely affected may seek compensation, and it is safe to say that customary international law recognizes this."*[221]

On the other hand, it has also been pointed out that compensation does not depend on demonstrating total loss of the property concerned. Despite the lack of any precise method of quantification, it seems that the international law threshold for compensation is somewhere between total deprivation of property rights and mere interference with the latter. However, arbitral tribunals have tended to require a precise degree of interference that is "substantial". In this regard, the arbitral tribunal in *Pope & Talbot* referred to a test that has subsequently been used by other arbitrators. The arbitrators stated as follows:

> *"[...] While it may sometimes be uncertain whether a particular interference with business activities amounts to an expropriation, the test is whether the property has been "taken" from the owner. Thus, the Harvard Draft defines the standard as requiring interference that would "justify an inference that the owner [...] will not be able to use, enjoy or dispose of the property [...]" The Restatement, in addressing the question whether regulation may be considered expropriation, speaks of "action that is confiscatory, or that prevents,*

*unreasonably interferes with, or unduly delays, effective enjoyment of alien's property."
Indeed, at the hearing, the Investor's Counsel conceded, correctly, that under international
law, expropriation requires "substantial deprivation" [...]"*[222]

A related question is how arbitral tribunals come to the conclusion that in a particular case there has
been substantial deprivation. ISDS practice has followed an analysis comparing the investment's original
situation with its state after the challenged measures had been taken. This comparison enables arbitral
tribunals to examine the extent to which the bundle of ownership rights of the investor has been impaired.
For instance, in the *Methanex* case the basis for the tribunal to find that there was no regulatory
expropriation was the fact that the claimant had retained control over its assets, including subsidiaries and
manufacturing capabilities. Furthermore, although the claimant argued that it had lost customer base,
goodwill and market share, the tribunal considered that those variables standing alone could not amount
to expropriation. Referring to a similar finding of the arbitral tribunal in *Feldman v. Mexico*,[223] the
arbitrators stated in *Methanex*:

> "*Methanex* [has not] *established that the California ban manifested any of the features
> associated with expropriation. In Feldman v. Mexico, the tribunal held that: "[...] the
> regulatory action has not deprived the Claimant of control of his company, [...] interfered
> directly in the internal operations [...] or displaced the Claimant as the controlling
> shareholder. The claimant is free to pursue other continuing lines of business activity [...]. Of
> course, he was effectively precluded from exporting cigarettes [...]. However, this does not
> amount to Claimant's deprivation of control of his company." Methanex claims that it lost
> customer base, goodwill and market share [...]. In the view of the Tribunal, items such as
> goodwill and market share may [...] "constitute [...] an element of the value of an enterprise
> and as such may have been covered by some of the compensation payments". Hence in a
> comprehensive taking, these items may figure in valuation. But it is difficult to see how they
> might stand alone, in a case like the one before the Tribunal.*"[224]

A third element often considered by arbitral tribunals to determine whether a regulatory taking has
taken place is whether a particular measure implemented by a host country has negatively affected the
investor's reasonable "investment-backed expectations". ISDS practice has also taken into account
governmental regulatory interference in the economic sector in which the investor operates.[225] Within this
logic, investment-backed expectations of the investor constitute another factor in considering whether the
degree of interference with the rights of ownership is substantial enough to amount to an indirect
expropriation.

For instance, in *Metalclad v. Mexico*, the dispute involved measures to prevent the claimant from
using land as an underground landfill, and a subsequent decree establishing that land as a State wildlife
protected area. These measures were implemented despite the previous authorization granted to the
investor by the federal authorities to build the landfill. The arbitral tribunal stated that "*expropriation* [...]
includes [...] *interference with property which has the effect of depriving the owner, in whole or significant
part, of the use or reasonably-to-be-expected economic benefit of the property* [...]."[226]

The reasonable expectations of the investor may also be a factor actually serving the interests of the
respondent host country. The dispute in *Olguin v. Republic of Paraguay*[227] illustrates this point. This case
arose out of the bankruptcy of a bank in Paraguay. The claimant, a Peruvian investor, alleged that the
actions of the financial authorities of Paraguay had led to the bankruptcy of the bank and thus prejudice to
him. The tribunal noted that the claimant was an experienced businessman who was aware of the
administrative situation in Paraguay and that he had made a risky and speculative investment. Thus, the
actual knowledge of local circumstances, and the degree of risk voluntarily undertaken by the investor in
the light of that knowledge were found to be a key element in denying the existence of an indirect
expropriation in this case.

Furthermore, in *Olguin*, the tribunal noted that although the government accounting bodies charged with the oversight of banking services were negligent in performing their duties,[228] an expropriation could not be materialized through acts of omission. In the tribunal's view, expropriation requires positive acts of government.[229]

Metalclad illustrates another important element in the analysis of arbitration awards on regulatory expropriations. That is, the focus of the enquiry is whether the challenged measure has had the effect of depriving the investor of its ownership rights. In this regard, the reason for the measure – in *Metalclad*, the protection of the environment – is not particularly relevant. Arbitral tribunals, as in *Compañia de Desarrollo de Santa Elena S.A. v. Costa Rica*, have stated that:

> "*Expropriatory environmental measures – no matter how laudable and beneficial to society as a whole – are, in this respect, similar to any other expropriatory measures that a state may take in order to implement its policies: where property is expropriated, even for environmental purposes, whether domestic or international, the state's obligation to pay compensation remains.*"[230]

In the same direction, the Tribunal in *Tecmed v. Mexico* stated that regulatory measures are covered by the same rules on expropriation as other types of government measures. As in most other recent cases, the effect on the investor was considered to be the primary test to apply. This includes the economic impact and a test that considers the loss of rights of the investor.[231] However, the tribunal seems to have set a particularly high bar for the degree of impact in this case, asking whether the "*negative economic impact of such actions on the financial position of the investor is sufficient to neutralize in full the value, or economic or commercial use of its investment without receiving any compensation whatsoever*".[232]

Although not very frequent, another element applied in some recent arbitration cases concerning regulatory takings is an examination of the proportionality between the public policy objective pursued by the challenged measure and the impact of such measure on the property of the investor. If the individual owner of the property has to bear a burden, which is too heavy in the light of the aim to be achieved, the measure is deemed to be disproportionate and thus more likely to lead to a finding that there was a taking of property subject to compensation.[233] This approach has frequently been used in the jurisprudence of the European Court of Human Rights, and it is not until recently that some ISDS arbitral tribunals started to apply it.

One of the few investment disputes in which a proportionality test has been recently used among the elements to determine whether a regulatory taking had in fact occurred is the decision in *Tecmed v. Mexico*. After finding that there had been a practically total deprivation of property rights of the investor, the tribunal undertook an analysis of the proportionality of the challenged measures:

> "*After establishing that regulatory actions and measures will not be initially excluded from the definition of expropriatory acts, in addition to the negative financial impact of such actions or measures, the Arbitral Tribunal will consider, in order to determine if they are to be characterized as expropriatory, whether such actions or measures are proportional to the public interest presumably protected thereby and to the protection legally granted to investments, taking into account that the significance of such impact has a key role upon deciding the proportionality.*"[234]

In conclusion, through the use of the various tests referred to above, ISDS practice is gradually developing a body of jurisprudence to deal with the issue of regulatory takings. Through these tests, most arbitral tribunals have established a threshold requirement for a compensable expropriation that, in fact, rules out for the majority of the complaints that an indirect expropriation through economic regulation by the State has occurred. However, despite the evolving jurisprudence and guidance in this regard, tribunals have not yet developed a clear analytical framework that Governments may use in order to determine whether an envisaged measure constitutes an acceptable regulation or amounts to a regulatory taking requiring compensation. Although it is clear that more and more tribunals require that there be a substantial deprivation of property rights, the question of "substantial" and the definition of what is "property" remain unclear.

6.   Other provisions

Besides the provisions discussed above, IIAs contain other obligations, such as the freedom of capital movements, prohibition on certain performance requirements being imposed on foreign investors, and provisions allowing for the movement of top managerial personnel. However, among those other possible grounds for submitting a claim under ISDS procedures, it appears that over the last decade only that concerning the prohibition of performance requirements has been invoked in ISDS practice. This finding applies only to NAFTA's Chapter 11, since with few exceptions[235] most BITs do not contain any provision on performance requirements.

Three disputes concerning the issue of performance requirements are salient in the NAFTA context: *S.D. Myers v. Canada*, *Pope & Talbot v. Canada* and *ADF v. United States*.

In *S.D. Myers*, the dispute involved a ban on toxic waste (PCB) exports imposed by Canada that affected a United States company whose business consisted in exporting such waste from Canada to be processed in Ohio. The claimant argued, inter alia, that the PCB export ban breached Article 1106 of NAFTA because, in effect, it required that the claimant carry out the disposal of PCBs in Canada. Such a requirement entailed, in the view of the claimant, the consumption of goods and services in Canada that otherwise would not need to be consumed. A majority of the tribunal held that the ban did not breach Article 1106 because it did not impose any specific requirement on S.D. Myers in relation to Canadian goods or services or to achieve a given level of Canadian content.[236]

A more detailed analysis of Article 1106 was undertaken by the arbitral tribunal in *Pope & Talbot*. As explained above, this dispute involved a form of tariff-rate export restraint devised by Canada to comply with the terms of a voluntary export restraint agreement negotiated with the United States on softwood lumber. That regime allocated to softwood lumber producers in certain provinces a quota of lumber that they could export duty-free, and imposed a scale of fees on lumber exported above the quota. The investor challenged the Canadian measures, inter alia, on the ground that they were designed to impose a requirement to export a given percentage of goods. The tribunal held that the quota scheme did not impose any export requirement on investors. It also found that the regime did not impose a restriction or limitation on domestic sales of softwood lumber within the meaning of Article 1106.[237]

Another more recent case in which a violation of Article 1106 was claimed is *ADF Group Inc. v. United States*. The dispute involved a grant made by the United States Federal Government to the State of Virginia to undertake a highway construction project. The grant was subject to the requirement that the State of Virginia would adopt the protectionist standards used in the "Federal Buy America Act" for any procurements made under the highway project. Under that legislation, only products of United States origin can benefit from government procurement contracts. ADF was employed as a subcontractor to provide steel. Because the steel used by ADF was of Canadian origin, ADF was dropped from the project. ADF claimed, inter alia, that that measure breached Article 1106, as it forced providers to use only domestic goods. The tribunal found that under Article 1108 of NAFTA government procurement by a contracting party was exempted from the obligations on performance requirements and that the grant conditions were essentially contained in the definition of a "procurement" measure. Consequently, there was no breach of Article 1106 because of the exclusion set out in Article 1108.[238]

It can be concluded that the decisions in *S.D. Myers*, *Pope & Talbot* and *ADF* are consistent with the primary rationale of Article 1106, which is to ensure that investment approvals or access to government benefits, like subsidies, are not linked to specific performance requirements that will have a distorting effect on trade in goods. A factor explaining why no arbitral tribunal has so far found a breach of Article 1106 of NAFTA could be that according to Article 1106(5) prohibitions under Article 1106(1) and (3) "*do not apply to any requirement other than the requirements set out in those paragraphs*". In other words, the prohibition on performance requirements is limited to the closed list in Article 1106.   The three cases mentioned have interpreted those provisions in a consistent manner.

Notes

[1] *Asian Agricultural Products Ltd. v. Republic of Sri Lanka*, ICSID Case No. ARB/87/3, 27 June 1990. Note: unless otherwise indicated, all cases can be found on the ICSID webpage at www.worldbank.org/icsid/cases/cases.htm, or at http://ita.law.uvic.ca/chronological_list.htm.

[2] The figures referred to in this section are, with minor exceptions, mainly based on published NAFTA and ICSID cases, and take account only of those arbitral decisions – both preliminary and final awards – that are publicly available.

[3] The sole known exception is a 2003 State-to-State dispute between Chile and Peru that was lodged in response to an investor–State claim filed by a Chilean firm, Lucchetti (*Lucchetti S.A. and Lucchetti Peru S.A. v. Republic of Peru*, ICSID Case No. ARB/03/4). The State–State procedure was discontinued, and the investor–State case was only recently decided. In other instances, States have set up claims commissions to deal with investor-to-State cases, such as the Iran–United States Claims Tribunal.

[4] UNCTAD's database includes all claims that have been submitted to arbitration, including those that were settled after they had been registered.

[5] While the ICSID facility maintains a public registry of claims, other arbitral mechanisms do not. Hence, no official records of all claims filed are available. Furthermore, in some cases the investors or Governments involved in a dispute wish to keep the dispute confidential, with the result that the disputants themselves do not reveal the existence of a claim.

[6] The worldwide inward FDI stock more than tripled between 1995 and 2005 (from $2.8 trillion at the end of 1995 to $10.1 trillion at the end of 2005); see www.unctad.org/wir.

[7] In UNCTAD's database, the "beef cases" against the United States are counted as one case, rather than 100, following the United States practice on its website. Furthermore, all of these cases pertain to the same facts and the same treaty. By contrast, the seven "Dabhol banks cases" are counted as individual cases, because they pertain to the same facts, but different investment treaties.

[8] There are important exceptions to this trend, however. As will be explained in section III, ISDS is one of the key areas where there have been significant developments in treaty making over the last decade.

[9] ICISD Case No. ARB/02/9, Decision on Jurisdiction, 21 October 2003.

[10] *Nottebohm Case* (Liechtenstein v. Guatemala), ICJ, 1955.

[11] Iran–United States Claims Tribunal, Case N° A/18 of 6 April 1984 (5 Iran-U.S.C.T.R.-251).

[12] However, the tribunal did not rule out the possibility that situations might arise where the exclusion of dual nationals could lead to a result that was manifestly absurd or unreasonable (Vienna Convention, Article (32)(b)): "*One could envisage a situation where a country continues to apply the jus sanguinis over many generations. It might for instance be questionable if the third or fourth foreign born generation, which has no ties whatsoever with the country of its forefathers, could still be considered to have, for the purpose of the Convention, the nationality of this state*".

[13] ICSID Case No. ARB/02/7, Award, 7 July 2004.

[14] Ibid., para. 55.

[15] For instance, the BIT between the United States and Uruguay (2005) provides that an "*"investor of a Party" means a Party or state enterprise thereof, or a national or an enterprise of a Party, that attempts to make, is making, or has made an investment in the territory of the other Party; provided, however, that a natural person who is a dual citizen shall be deemed to be exclusively a citizen of the State of his or her dominant and effective citizenship*".

[16] An example is the BIT between Argentina and Canada, which states as follows:
"*The term "investor" includes any natural person who makes the investment possessing the citizenship or* **permanently** *residing in a Contracting Party in accordance with its laws*" (emphasis added).

[17] For a detailed discussion of this particular trend, see Schreuer 2001.

[18] ICISD Case No. ARB/84/3, Decision on Jurisdiction, 27 November 1985.

[19] ICSID Case No. ARB/74/3, Decision on Jurisdiction, 6 July 1975.

[20] ICSID Case No. ARB/02/18, Decision on Jurisdiction, 29 April 2004.

[21] ICSID Case No. ARB/00/5, Decision on Jurisdiction, 27 September 2001.

[22] Legal doctrine has recognized that definitions of corporate nationality in IIAs providing for ICSID's jurisdiction will apply for determining whether the nationality requirements of Article 25(2)(b) have been met, as they are part of the legal framework for the host country's submission to the Centre. In this regard, "[…] *any reasonable determination of the nationality of juridical persons contained in national legislation or in a treaty should be accepted by an ICSID commission or tribunal*" (Schreuer 2001).

[23] For instance, the BIT between Mexico and the Netherlands explicitly provides for this possibility in its definition of "investor". Article 1, paragraph 3, of the Agreements provides as follows:
"*(3) the term "nationals" shall comprise with regard to either Contracting Party:*
(a) natural persons having the nationality of that Contracting Party;
(b) legal persons constituted under the law of that Contracting Party;
(c) legal persons constituted under the law of the other Contracting Party but controlled, directly or indirectly, by natural persons as defined in (a) or by legal persons as defined in (b) above."

[24] An example of this approach is NAFTA Article 1117, the relevant part of which reads as follows:
"*Article 1117: Claim by an Investor of a Party on Behalf of an Enterprise*
1. An investor of a Party, on behalf of an enterprise of another Party that is a juridical person that the investor owns or controls directly or indirectly, may submit to arbitration under this Section a claim that the other Party has breached an obligation under: (a) Section A […]."

[25] ICSID Case No. ARB/83/2, Award, 31 March 1986.

[26] ICSID Case No. ARB/81/2, Award, 21 October 1983.

27 ICSID Case No. ARB/81/1, Award, 20 November 1984.

28 ICSID Case No. ARB/81/1, Decision on Jurisdiction, 25 September 1983, cited in Schreuer 2001, para. 513.

29 It should be noted, however, that in contexts different from ICSID, arbitral tribunals have also considered variables other than share ownership in order to determine whether an investor controls a legal entity. In *S.D.Myers Inc. v. Canada*, an UNCITRAL procedure brought under NAFTA chapter 11, the claim of the investor was challenged on the basis that the investor did not own shares in the investment in question and, consequently, was not a covered investor under NAFTA. The Tribunal nevertheless found that S.D. Myers Inc., the United States investor, controlled Myers Canada not through legal ownership of shares, but on the basis that Mr. Dana Myers, who was President of S.D.Myers Inc., in fact controlled every decision, investment and transaction made by Myers Canada. See *S.D.Myers Inc. v. Canada*, UNCITRAL, First Partial Award, 13 November 2000, available at (http://www.investmentclaims.com/decisions/SDMyers-Canada-1stPartialAward-13Nov2000.pdf).

30 ICSID Case No. ARB/81/2, Award, 21 October 1983.

31 ICSID Case No. ARB/83/2, Decision on Jurisdiction, 24 October 1984.

32 ICSID Case No. ARB/92/1, Award, 16 February 1994.

33 ICSID Case No. ARB/82/1, Decision on Jurisdiction, 1 August 1984.

34 ICISD Case No. ARB/02/9, Decision on Jurisdiction, 21 October 2003.

35 ICSID Case No. ARB(AF)/98/3, Award on Merits, 26 June 2003.

36 In this regard it has been affirmed that "[a]*ny change in the juridical person's nationality after the date of consent is immaterial for jurisdiction. Subsequent to consent, a juridical person may lose the nationality of the original Contracting State and may acquire the nationality of a non-Contracting State or that of the host State without losing access to ICSID*" (Schreuer 2001, para. 493).

37 Mendelson 2005, pp. 147–148.

38 *Case Concerning the Barcelona Traction, Light and Power Company, Limited* (Belgium v. Spain), 5 February 1970 (1970) I.C.J.3 at 35–36, 9 I.L.M. 227.

39 ICSID Case No. ARB/02/1, Decision on Jurisdiction, 30 April 2004.

40 ICSID Case No. ARB/01/8, Decision on Jurisdiction, 17 July 2003.

41 ICSID Case No. ARB/02/8, Decision on Jurisdiction, 3 August 2004.

42 ICSID Case No. ARB/01/12, Decision on Jurisdiction, 8 December 2003.

43 ICSID Case No. ARB/01/8, Decision on Jurisdiction, 17 July 2003, para. 45.

44 Ibid., para. 48.

45 Ibid., para. 51.

46 ICSID Case No. ARB/97/6, Decision on Jurisdiction, 8 December 1998.

47 ICSID Case No. ARB/01/8, Decision on Jurisdiction, 17 July 2003, para. 63.

48 For instance, in *GAMI Investments Inc. v. Mexico*, the investor held only a 14.8 per cent equity interest in the investment. See Final Award, 15 November 2004, UNCITRAL, available at the website of the Ministry of Economy of Mexico (http://www.economia.gob.mx/work/snci/negociaciones/Controversias/Casos_Mexico/Gami).

49 ICSID Case No. ARB/97/7, Decision on Jurisdiction, 25 January 2000.

50 Ibid., para. 79.

51 Ibid., paras. 80–81.

52 ICSID Case No. ARB/00/4, Decision on Jurisdiction, 23 July 2001.

53 Ibid., para. 32.

54 Furthermore, some IIAs contain "umbrella clauses" which have the effect of significantly expanding the scope of application of ISDS mechanisms under the agreement. The jurisprudence on umbrella clauses and their implications will be specifically addressed in the section on investment treaty arbitration and jurisdiction over contract claims (subsection B.1d).

55 Among the numerous IIAs following this approach are the BIT between the Russian Federation and Ethiopia (2000), the BIT between Indonesia and Morocco (1997), the BIT between Japan and Bangladesh (1998) and the BIT between Chile and Austria (1997).

56 The ICJ has defined a dispute as "*a disagreement on a point of law or fact, a conflict of legal views or interests between parties*", Case concerning East Timor, 1995 ICJ Reports, 89.

57 Schreuer 2001, para. 71.

58 Ibid., para. 42.

59 ICSID Case No. ARB/96/3(1), Decision on Jurisdiction, 11 July 1997.

60 Ibid., para. 24.

61 Schreuer 2001, para. 71.

62 The complexities related to investment treaty arbitration and jurisdiction over contract claims will be developed in sub-section B.1.d.

63 ICSID Case No.ARB/72/1, Decision on Jurisdiction, 12 May 1974. Cited in Schreuer 2001, para. 71.

64 For instance, the BIT between Saudi Arabia and Malaysia (2000), besides domestic courts, refers only to ICSID as an alternative venue for investor-related disputes.

65 *Methanex Corporation v. United States*, UNCITRAL, Preliminary Award on Jurisdiction and Admissibility, 7 August 2002, para. 147.

66 In this regard, it has been noted that "[i]*n agreeing to ICSID arbitration, the parties would be left to determine the kinds of activity which could give rise to a dispute contemplated in Article 25(1). In other words, consent of the parties in a particular case implied their recognition that the investment criteria had been met.*" (Hamida 2005, p. 53).

67 In some NAFTA cases, arbitral tribunals – established under UNCITRAL – have considered to be covered investments assets of an immaterial nature. That is the case in *Pope & Talbot v. Canada*, where the tribunal found that market shares through

trade could be regarded as part of the assets of an investment, or in *S.D.Myers v. Canada*, where the tribunal held that the establishment of a sales office and commitment or marketing time formed a sufficient investment. See *Pope & Talbot Inc. v. Canada*, UNCITRAL, Interim Award on the Merits, 26 June 2000, and *S.D.Myers Inc. v Canada*, UNCITRAL, First Partial Award, 13 November 2000.

[68] ICSID Case No. ARB/96/3(1), Decision on Jurisdiction, 11 July 1997.

[69] Ibid., para. 37.

[70] Ibid., para. 43.

[71] ICSID Case No. ARB/00/4, Decision on Jurisdiction, 23 July 2001.

[72] Ibid., para. 52.

[73] ICSID Case No. ARB/03/11, Decision on Jurisdiction, 6 August 2004.

[74] Ibid., para. 45.

[75] Ibid., para. 47.

[76] Ibid., para. 50.

[77] Ibid., para. 53.

[78] See, for instance, Article 10.1 of the BIT between Chile and New Zealand (1999), which states that "*Any dispute between a Contracting Party and an investor of the other Contracting Party shall, as far as possible, be settled amicably through negotiations between the parties to the dispute*".

[79] For example, Article 15.1 of the BIT between Japan and the Republic of Korea (2002) provides that "*For purposes of this Article, an investment dispute is a dispute between a Contracting Party and an investor of the other Contracting Party that has incurred loss or damage by reason of, or arising out of, an alleged breach of any right conferred by this Agreement with respect to an investment of an investor of that other Contracting Party*".

[80] In this regard, see Gaillard 2005, p. 3.

[81] For instance, in *Compañía del Aguas del Aconquija, S.A.& Compagnie Générale des Eaux v. Argentina* (the *Vivendi I Case*), both the arbitral tribunal and the ad hoc committee that had to decide on the request for annulment of the award distinguished between claims based on the applicable IIA – the BIT between France and Argentina – and claims based on the concession contract. In this regard, the ad hoc committee found it "[…] *evident that a particular investment dispute may at the same time involve issues of the interpretation and application of the BIT's standards and questions of contract* […]". However, the committee also pointed out that a breach of a contract and a breach of the treaty entailed independent standards, and thus affirmed that "[a] *State may breach a treaty without breaching a contract, and vice versa*". Consequently, the committee stated that "[…] *whether there has been a breach of the BIT and whether there has been a breach of the contract are different questions*". ICSID Case No. ARB/97/3, Annulment Tribunal, Decision on Annulment, 3 July 2002. The distinction between treaty-based claims and contract-based claims has also been upheld in numerous other cases, such as in *LANCO v. Argentina* (ICSID Case No. ARB/07/6), *Azurix Corporation v. Argentina* (ICSID Case No. ARB/01/12) and *CMS v. Argentina* (ICSID Case No. ARB/01/8), among others.

[82] For instance, see *Azinian v. Mexico*, ICSID Case No. ARB(AF)/97/2, Award, 1 November 1999; *Mondev v. United States*, ICSID Case No. ARB(AF)/99/2, Award, 11 October 2002; *Waste Management v. Mexico*, ICSID Case No. ARB(AF)/00/3, Award, 30 April 2004; *Amco v. Indonesia*, ICSID Case No. ARB/81/1, Award, 20 November 1984; and *LETCO v. Liberia*, ICSID Case No. ARB/83/2, Award,   31 March 1986.

[83] Article 8 of the Italy–Morocco BIT reads as follows: "*All disputes or differences, including disputes related to the amount of compensation due in the event of expropriation, nationalisation, or similar measures, between a Contracting Party and an investor of the other Contracting Party concerning an investment of the said investor on the territory of the first Contracting Party* […]".

[84] In this regard, the *Salini v. Morocco* tribunal held: "[…] the Tribunal considers that its scope of application regarding the nature of the disputes is limited as to the persons concerned. In the case where the State has organised a sector of activity through a distinct legal entity, be it a State entity, it does not necessarily follow that the State has accepted a priori that the jurisdiction offer contained in Article 8 should bind it with respect to contractual breaches committed by this entity. […] In other words, Article 8 compels the State to respect the jurisdiction offer in relation to violations of the Bilateral Treaty and any breach of a contract that binds the State directly. The jurisdiction offer contained in Article 8 does not, however, extend to breaches of a contract to which an entity other than the State is a named party". ICSID Case No. ARB/00/4, Decision on Jurisdiction, 23 July 2001, paras. 60 and 61.

[85] As the contract involved an Italian investor and a Pakistani public – but autonomous corporate – body, legally and financially distinct from Pakistan, the tribunal decided that it lacked jurisdiction under the BIT between Italy and Pakistan to entertain Impregilo's claims based on alleged breaches of the contracts. See *Impregilo S.p.A v. Pakistan*, ICSID Case No. ARB/02/2, Decision on Jurisdiction, 22 April 2005, paras. 198–211.

[86] ICSID Case No. ARB/97/3, Decision on Annulment, 3 July 2002, para. 55.

[87] ICSID Case No. ARB/02/6, Decision on Jurisdiction, 29 January 2004, paras. 131–135.

[88] ICSID Case No. ARB/01/13, Decision on Jurisdiction, 6 August 2003.

[89] Ibid., para. 161.

[90] ICSID Case No. ARB/03/8, Award, 10 January 2005.

[91] Ibid., para. 25.

[92] In this regard, see Schreuer 2005, p. 299.

[93] ICSID Case No. ARB/01/13, Decision on Jurisdiction, 6 August 2003.

[94] ICSID Case No. ARB/03/11, Decision on Jurisdiction, 6 August 2004.

[95] ICSID Case No. ARB/02/6, Decision on Jurisdiction, 29 January 2004.

[96] ICSID Case No. ARB/03/8, Award, 10 January 2005.

97   Partial Award, 19 August 2005, Ad hoc arbitration procedure, available at (http://www.investmentclaims.com/decisions/ Eureko-Poland-LiabilityAward.pdf).

98   ICSID Case No. ARB/01/13, Decision on Jurisdiction, 6 August 2003, para. 167.

99   ICSID Case No. ARB/03/11, Decision on Jurisdiction, 6 August 2004, para. 81.

100   ICSID Case No. ARB/02/6, Decision on Jurisdiction, 29 January 2004, para. 128.

101   Ibid., para. 127.

102   Despite finding that it had jurisdiction over both treaty and contract claims, the arbitral tribunal in *SGS v. Philippines* declined to proceed on the merits and instead referred the parties to the domestic courts for the determination of the amount due. It has been recognized that this refraining from exercising jurisdiction is similar to what the *Vivendi I* tribunal did, which constituted the grounds for annulling the award. However, in *SGS v. Philippines* the decision was not made in the form of an award – such a decision being under the ICSID Convention the only decision subject to annulment – but in the form of a decision on jurisdiction, leaving the claimants with no recourse against that decision.

103   ICSID Case No. ARB/03/8, Award, 10 January 2005, para. 25. Translation from the award in French, cited in Schreuer 2005.

104   ICSID Case No. ARB(AF)/00/3, Arbitral Award, 26 May 2000.

105   Ibid., para. 27.

106   ICSID Case No. ARB/01/8, Decision on Jurisdiction, 17 July 2003.

107   ICSID Case No. ARB/99/2, Award, 25 June 2001.

108   ICSID Case No. ARB/97/3, Decision on Annulment, 3 July 2002.

109   ICSID Case No. ARB(AF)/98/5, Decision on Jurisdiction, 8 August 2000.

110   ICSID Case No. ARB/01/8, Decision on Jurisdiction, 17 July 2003, para. 80.

111   ICISD Case No. ARB/77/2, Award, 8 August 1989, para. 1.14, cited in *Azurix Corp. v. Argentina*, ICSID Case No. ARB/01/12, Decision on Jurisdiction, 8 December 2003, para. 88.

112   ICSID Case No. ARB/01/12, Decision on Jurisdiction, 8 December 2003.

113   ICISD Case No. ARB/01/3, Decision on Jurisdiction, 14 January 2004.

114   ICISD Case No. ARB/02/1, Decision on Jurisdiction, 30 April 2004.

115   See *Compañiá de Aguas del Aconquija & Vivendi Universal (formerly Compagnie Générale des Eaux) v. Argentine Republic*, ICSID Case No. ARB/97/3, Decision on Annulment, 3 July 2002. An example of multiple cases brought by different investors and the investment is also *Alex Genin, Eastern Credit Limited v. Republic of Estonia*, ICSID Case No. ARB/99/2, Award, 25 June 2001, paras. 331–333; see also *Ronald Lauder v. Czech Republic*, UNCITRAL, Final Award, 3 September 2001, para. 163; *Enron and Ponderosa Assets v. Argentine Republic*, ICSID Case No. ARB/01/3, Decision on Jurisdiction, 14 January 2004, para. 98; *Azurix Corp. v. Argentine Republic*, ICSID Case No. ARB/01/12, Decision on Jurisdiction, 8 December 2003, para. 90; and *CMS Gas Transmission Company v. Argentine Republic*, ICSID Case ARB/01/8, Award, 12 May 2005, para. 80.

116   See UNCTAD 2005a, pp. 20–21.

117   These disputes involved a common set of facts and measures, namely alleged improper interference by the Czech Government in the investors' investments in the television business. One such investor lost its case, but the other won an award of over $300 million. See UNCTAD 2005a, p. 19.

118   See *Ronald S. Lauder v. Czech Republic*, UNCITRAL, Final Award, 3 September 2001; *CME Czech Republic B.V. v. Czech Republic*, UNCITRAL, Partial Award, 13 September 2001; and *The Czech Republic v. CME Czech Republic B.V*, Court of Appeals, Stockholm, Sweden, Case No. T-8735-01   (42 *International Legal Materials* 919 (2003)).

119   ICSID Case No. ARB(AF)/04/1.

120   ICSID Case No. ARB(AF)/04/5.

121   Order of the Consolidation Tribunal, 20 May 2005, paras. 8, 9 and 15.

122   *Canfor Corp. v. United States of America*, *Terminal Forest Products Ltd. v. United States of America* and *Tembec Inc. et al. v. United States of America*, Order of the Consolidation Tribunal, 7 September 2005, at http://naftaclaims.com/ Disputes/USA/ Softwood/Softwood-ConOrder.pdf.

123   Order of the Consolidation Tribunal, 7 September 2005, paras. 109–114.

124   In paragraph 221 of the order of consolidation the tribunal stated the following:
      "*The Consolidation Tribunal concludes that all four conditions of Article 1126(2) of the NAFTA are met in the present proceedings. First, it is common ground that the claims in question have been submitted to arbitration under Article 1120. Second, the Tribunal has found that many questions of law and fact are common in the three Article 1120 arbitrations. Third, the Tribunal has also found that the interests of fair and efficient resolution of the claims merit the assumption of jurisdiction over all of the claims. And fourth, the parties to the present proceedings have been heard.*"

125   In paragraph 222 of the order of consolidation, the tribunal stated the following:
      "*The result in the present case differs from the one in the Corn Products case. There are several reasons for the different outcome, which include the following. First, the Order on Consolidation in* Corn Products *is silent about what Article 1126(2) requires for satisfying the term "a question of law or fact in common". [...] Second, as a general proposition, the present Tribunal disagrees with the statements found in § 9 of the* Corn Products *Order: "Two tribunals can handle two separate cases more fairly and efficiently than one tribunal where the two claimants are direct and major competitors, and the claims raise issues of competitive and commercial sensitivity," [...] Third, [...] While the present case involves also common questions of law and fact relating to jurisdiction, the same applies to liability as well, in respect of which the United States has raised, and intends to raise, common questions of law and fact. Moreover, in the judgment of the present Tribunal, anticipated questions may also be taken into account if there is a degree of certainty that they will be raised. Fourth, while acknowledging the risk of inconsistent awards, in § 16 of the* Corn Products *Order, it is stated that: "This Tribunal does not have before it a large number of identically or very similarly situated claimants. [...] The tax could, for example, constitute an expropriation as to one claimant, but not another." This fact pattern does not apply to the present*

case. Lastly, in § 19, the <u>Corn Products</u> *Order emphasizes that the cases there "are not close to procedural alignment," which is not applicable in the present case either."*

[126] See http://www.worldbank.org/icsid/cases/cases.htm.

[127] Amendment to Arbitration Rule 48, ICSID 2004.

[128] ICSID Case No. ARB/02/3, Decision on Jurisdiction, 21 October 2005.

[129] Ibid., para. 17.

[130] Ibid.

[131] Ibid.

[132] ICSID Case No. ARB(AF)/97/1, Award, 30 August 2000, para. 13.

[133] ICSID Case No. ARB(AF)/98/3, Award on Jurisdiction, 5 January 2001, para. 26.

[134] UNCITRAL, Decision on *Amici Curiae*, 15 January 2001.

[135] UNICTRAL, Award on Jurisdiction, 22 November 2002.

[136] See (http://www.worldbank.org/icsid/cases/cases.htm). Statement of the NAFTA Free Trade Commission of 31 July 2001 (http://www.dfait-maeci.gc.ca/tna-nac/NAFTA-Interpr-en.asp).

[137] See UNCTAD 1999a; 1999b.

[138] NAFTA, Articles 1101–1102, Annexes I, II, III and IV. Chapter 6 of NAFTA is also of relevance to the energy sector, and Chapter 14 is relevant for financial services.

[139] ICSID Case No. ARB/00/2, Award, 15 March 2002.

[140] ICISD Case No. ARB/00/1, unpublished. For an analysis of this case, see Hamida 2005, p. 67.

[141] Stockholm Chamber of Commerce (SCC) Case 049/2002, between Mr. William Nagel and the Czech Republic, unpublished. Summary of the award published, without the parties being identified, in Stockholm Arbitration Report 2004, p. 141. For an analysis of this case, see Hamida 2005, p. 70.

[142] Since then, in addition to the cases that will be referred to below, there has been more authority on this point, though not as basic as in *Mihaly*. See *Generation Ukraine, Inc. v. Ukraine*, ICSID Case No. ARB/00/9, Award, 16 September 2003, paras 8.6, 18.5–18.9; and *PSEG Global, Inc., The North American Coal Corporation, and Konyalngin Electrik Uretim ve Ticaret Limited Sirketi v. Turkey*, ICSID Case No. ARB/02/5, Decision on Jurisdiction, 4 June 2004, paras. 67–105.

[143] ICSID Case No. ARB/00/2, Award, 15 March 2002, para. 11.

[144] Article 1 of the BIT between the United States and Sri Lanka reads as follows:
"*1. For the purposes of this Treaty,*
   (a) *"investment" means every kind of investment in the territory of one Party owned or controlled directly or indirectly by nationals or companies of the other Party, such as equity, debt, and service and investment contracts; and includes:*
      (i) *tangible and intangible property, including rights such as mortgages, liens and pledges;*
      (ii) *a company or shares of stock or other interests in a company or interests in the assets thereof;*
      (iii) *a claim to money or a claim to performance having economic value, and associated with an investment;*
      (iv) *intellectual property which includes, inter alia, rights relating to: literary and artistic works, including sound recordings, patentable inventions in all fields of human endeavor, industrial designs, semiconductor mask works, trade secrets, know-how, and confidential business information, and trademarks, service marks, and trade names; and*
      (v) *any right conferred by law or contract, and any licenses and permits pursuant to law;"*

[145] ICSID Case No.ARB/00/2, Award, 15 March 2002, paras. 58–61.

[146] See Hamida 2005, p. 69.

[147] Ibid., p. 68.

[148] Stockholm Chamber of Commerce (SCC) Case 049/2002, between Mr. William Nagel and the Czech Republic, unpublished. Summary of the award, published without the parties being identified, in Stockholm Arbitration Report 2004, p.141. For an analysis of this case, see Hamida 2005, p. 70.

[149] bid., p. 69.

[150] See UNCTAD 1998, p. 53.

[151] Many BITs, after providing for fair and equitable treatment, add explicitly that investment by the other contracting party should be provided with "full protection and security" or "most constant protection and security". Unlike in the case of the fair and equitable treatment standard, the content of the principle of full protection and security has been defined with more precision. As pointed out by UNCTAD (1998, p. 55), not only is this an old standard commonly used in Friendship, Commerce and Navigation (FCN) treaties, but also it was included in early BITs before the concept of fair and equitable treatment had been introduced. In this regard, it has been stated:
"*The provision does not impose strict liability on the host country to protect foreign investment. In effect, the standard does not represent a deviation from the due diligence rule. Thus, the term "full protection and security" connotes the assurance of full protection and security for foreign investors as contemplated or required by customary international law. At the same time, the clause on full protection and security is unusual in that it contemplates protecting investment against private as well as public action, that is, the clause requires that the host country should exercise reasonable care to protect investment against injury by private parties.*"

[152] "*Non-discrimination, in its general sense, means that the host country must abstain from discriminatory action towards foreign investors in general or towards specific groups of foreign investors. [...] Although arguably, the standard of fair and equitable treatment implicitly excludes arbitrary or discriminatory treatment, some BITs explicitly prohibit such treatment.*" Ibid.

[153] For a detailed explanation of this position, see UNCTAD 1999c, pp. 37–41; and UNCTAD 2007.

[154] Article 1105(1) of NAFTA reads as follows:

"1. Each Party shall accord to investment of investors of another Party treatment in accordance with international law, including fair and equitable treatment and full protection and security."

155   ICSID Case No. ARB(AF)/97/1, Award, 30 August 2000.

156   UNCITRAL, First Partial Award, 13 November 2000.

157   UNCITRAL, Award on the Merits, 10 April 2001.

158   In this regard, the *Metalclad* tribunal concluded that:
"Mexico failed to ensure a transparent and predictable framework for Metalclad's business planning and investment. The totality of these circumstances demonstrates a lack of orderly process and timely disposition in relation to an investor of a Party acting in the expectation that it would be treated fairly and justly in accordance with the NAFTA."
ICSID Case No. ARB(AF)/97/1, Award, 30 August 2000, para. 99.

159   Review by the British Columbia Supreme Court (2001 BCSC 664), 2 May 2001.

160   UNCITRAL, First Partial Award, 13 November 2000.

161   UNCITRAL, Award on the Merits, 10 April 2001, para. 110.

162   The relevant part of the Note of Interpretation issued by the Free Trade Commission states as follows:
"Having reviewed the operation of proceedings conducted under Chapter Eleven of the North American Free Trade Agreement, the Free Trade Commission hereby adopts the following interpretations of Chapter Eleven in order to clarify and reaffirm the meaning of certain of its provisions: [...]
B.   Minimum Standard of Treatment in Accordance with International Law
1.   Article 1105(1) prescribes the customary international law minimum standard of treatment of aliens as the minimum standard of treatment to be afforded to investments of investors of another Party.
2.   The concepts of "fair and equitable treatment" and "full protection and security" do not require treatment in addition to or beyond that which is required by the customary international law minimum standard of treatment of aliens.
3.   A determination that there has been a breach of another provision of the NAFTA, or of a separate international agreement, does not establish that there has been a breach of Article 1105(1)."
Note of Interpretation of the NAFTA Free Trade Commission, 31 July 2001.

163   ICSID Case No. ARB(AF)/99/2, Award, 11 October 2002, para. 119. In *ADF Group v. United States of America*, which concerned a statute on local procurement requirements, the tribunal reiterated the approach taken in *Mondev*, namely that a tribunal did not have carte blanche to arrive at its own idiosyncratic assessment, but must ground its determination in relevant sources of international law. ICSID Case No. ARB(AF)/00/1, Final Award, 9 January 2003, paras. 184–185.

164   ICSID Case No. ARB(AF)/99/2, Award, 11 October 2002.

165   Ibid., paras. 116, 123 and 125.

166   ICSID Case No. ARB(AF)/00/1, Final Award, 9 January 2003, para. 179.

167   ICSID Case No. ARB(AF)/98/3, Award on the Merits, 26 June 2003.

168   Ibid., para. 132.

169   ICSID Case No. ARB(AF)/00/3, Final Award, 30 April 2004.

170   Ibid., paras. 98–99.

171   UNCITRAL, Final Award, 15 November 2004, para. 103.

172   UNCITRAL, Final Award, 3 August 2005, Part IV, Chapter C, para. 14.

173   An example is the BIT between Argentina and the United States (1992), which reads as follows:
"ARTICLE II
[...] 2. a) Investment shall at all times be accorded fair and equitable treatment, shall enjoy full protection and security and shall in no case be accorded treatment less than that required by international law".

174   For instance, the BIT between Indonesia and Algeria (2000) provides as follows:
"Article III
Promotion and Protection of Investment"
[...] 2. Investments of investors of either Contracting Party shall at all times be accorded fair and equitable treatment and shall enjoy adequate protection and security in the territory of the other Contracting Party."

175   ICSID Case No. ARB/97/7, Award, 13 November 2000, para. 83.

176   ICSID Case No. ARB/99/6, Award 12 April 2002, para. 143.

177   ICSID Case No. ARB/99/2, Award, 25 June 2001, para. 367.

178   Article II.3(a) of the BIT between Estonia and United States provides as follows:
"Article II
[...] 3. (a) Investment shall at all times be accorded fair and equitable treatment, shall enjoy full protection and security and shall in no case be accorded treatment less than required by international law."

179   ICSID Case No. ARB(AF)/99/2), Award, 11 October 2002, para. 116.

180   ICSID Case No. ARB/01/8, Final Award, 12 May 2005.

181   ICSID Case No. ARB/01/12, Final Award, 14 July 2006, para. 364.

182   ICISD Case No. ARB(AF)/00/2, Final Award, 29 May 2003.

183   Ibid., para. 154.

184   ICSID Case No.ARB/01/8, Final Award, 12 May 2005, paras. 273–277.

185   See also *Waste Management Inc. v. the United Mexican States*, ICSID Case No. ARB(AF)/00/3, Final Award, 30 April 2004, para. 98.

186   See also, for example, *MTD Equity Sdn. Bhd. & MTD Chile S.A. v. Chile*, ICSID Case No.ARB/01/7, Final Award, 25 May 2004, and *Eudoro Armando Olguín v. Republic of Paraguay,* ICISD Case No.ARB/98/5, Final Award, 26 July 2001.

[187] The three leading BIT cases are *American Manufacturing & Trading v. Zaire*, ICISD Case No. ARB/93/1, Award, 21 February 1997; *Asian Agricultural Products Ltd. v. Republic of Sri Lanka*, ICSID Case No. ARB/87/3, Award, 27 June 1990; and *Wena Hotels Ltd v. Arab Republic of Egypt*, ICSID Case No. ARB/98/4, Award on Merits, 8 December 2000.

[188] *American Manufacturing & Trading v. Zaire*, ICSID Case No. ARB/93/1, Award, 21 February 1997 (reprinted in 12, *International Arbitration Reporter*, 1997, No. 4, pp. A-1 to A-2); *Asian Agricultural Products Ltd. v. Republic of Sri Lanka*, Award, 27 June 1990; and *Wena Hotel Ltd. v. Arab Republic of Egypt*, ICSID Case No. ARB/98/4, Decision on Jurisdiction, 29 June 1999; Award on Merits, 8 December 2000; and Decision on Annulment, 5 February 2002.

[189] See, for example, *CME Czech Republic B.V. v. Czech Republic*, UNCITRAL, Partial Award,   13 September 2001, para. 613; and *Ronald S. Lauder v. The Czech Republic*, UNCITRAL, Final Award, 3 September 2001, para. 314. See also *Jack Rankin v. The Islamic Republic of Iran*, Iran–United States Claims Tribunal, Award, 3 November 1987 (17 Iran–United States Claims Tribunal Reports), paras.   135 and 147.

[190] London Court of International Arbitration, Case No. UN 346, Award, 1 July 2004.

[191] Ibid., para. 187.

[192] ICISD Case No. ARB/01/12, Final Award, 14 July 2006.

[193] Ibid., para. 408.

[194] An example of this trend is the BIT between Japan and Viet Nam, Article 2.1 of which states as follows:
"*Article 2*
1.   *Each Contracting Party shall in its Area accord to investors of the other Contracting Party and to their investments treatment no less favourable than the treatment it accords* **in like circumstances** *to its own investors and their investments with respect to the establishment, acquisition, expansion, operation, management, maintenance, use, enjoyment, and sale or other disposal of investments (hereinafter referred to as "investment activities"). [...]*"
(emphasis added).

[195] UNCITRAL, Award on the Merits, 10 April 2001.

[196] Ibid., para. 78.

[197] ICSID Case No. ARB(AF)/99/1, Award on the Merits, 16 December 2002, para. 181.

[198] UNCITRAL, Final Award, 3 August 2005, Part IV, Chapter B, para. 19.

[199] Ibid., para. 14.

[200] UNCITRAL, First Partial Award, 13 November 2000, para. 252.

[201] Ibid., para. 254.

[202] ICSID Case No. ARB(AF)/99/1. Award on Merits, 16 December 2002, para. 181.

[203] Following this path of reasoning, the processes and production methods used to create a product, including their impact on the environment, have often been considered irrelevant to a determination of whether the products subject to comparison are in fact "like products". One of the most commented-on cases that followed this approach was the 1991 "Tuna Case", *United States-Restrictions on Imports of Tuna*, DS21/R (unadopted), 3 September 1991 (cited in GATT 1995, p. 138).

[204] UNCITRAL, Award on the Merits, 10 April 2001, para. 78.

[205] See, for example, *Asian Agricultural Products Limited v. Republic of Sri Lanka*, ICSID Case No. ARB/87/3, Award, 27 June 1990 (ICSID Reports 246); *Anglo-Iranian Oil Company Case*, International Court of Justice, Reports, 1952, p. 93; *Case concerning the rights of nationals of the United States of America in Morocco*, International Court of Justice, Reports, 1952, p. 176; and *Ambatielos Case*, International Court of Justice, Reports, 1953, p. 10.

[206] The first published case to address this is *Asian Agricultural Products Ltd. v. Republic of Sri Lanka*, ICSID Case No. ARB/87/3, Award, 27 June 1990 (ICSID Reports 246).

[207] ICSID Case No. ARB/97/7, Decision on Jurisdiction, 25 January 2000.

[208] The arbitral tribunal elaborated this point in greater detail and stated as follows: "*63. Here it is possible to envisage a number of situations not present in the instant case. First, if one contracting party has conditioned its consent to arbitration on the exhaustion of local remedies, which the ICSID Convention allows, this requirement could not be bypassed by invoking the most favored nation clause in relation to a third-party agreement that does not contain this element since the stipulated condition reflects a fundamental rule of international law. Second, if the parties have agreed to a dispute settlement arrangement which includes the so-called fork in the road, that is, a choice between submission to domestic courts or to international arbitration, and where the choice once made becomes final and irreversible, this stipulation cannot be bypassed by invoking the clause. This conclusion is compelled by the consideration that it would upset the finality of arrangements that many countries deem important as a matter of public policy. Third, if the agreement provides for a particular arbitration forum, such as ICSID, for example, this option cannot be changed by invoking the clause, in order to refer the dispute to a different system of arbitration. Finally, if the parties have agreed to a highly institutionalized system of arbitration that incorporates precise rules of procedure, which is the case, for example, with regard to the North America Free Trade Agreement and similar arrangements, it is clear that neither of these mechanisms could be altered by the operation of the clause because these very specific provisions reflect the precise will of the contracting parties. Other elements of public policy limiting the operation of the clause will no doubt be identified by the parties or tribunals. It is clear, in any event, that a distinction has to be made between the legitimate extension of rights and benefits by means of the operation of the clause, on the one hand, and disruptive treaty-shopping that would play havoc with the policy objectives of underlying specific treaty provisions, on the other hand*". Ibid.,   para. 63.

[209] ICSID Case No. ARB/02/8, Decision on Jurisdiction, 3 August 2004.

[210] Ibid., paras. 102 and 103.

[211] The reaction against extending MFN treatment to dispute settlement procedures is illustrated by the proposal made by several countries participating in the then active negotiations on the Free Trade of the Americas (FTAA). In the draft of 21 November 2003, a footnote 13 was included stating the following:

"Note: One delegation proposes the following footnote to be included in the negotiating history as a reflection of the Parties' shared understanding of the Most-Favored-Nation Article and the Maffezini case. This footnote would be deleted in the final text of the Agreement:

"The Parties note the recent decision of the arbitral tribunal in the Maffezini (Arg.) v. Kingdom of Spain, which found an unusually broad most favored nation clause in an Argentina-Spain agreement to encompass international dispute resolution procedures. See

Decision on Jurisdiction §§ 38-64 (January 25, 2000), reprinted in 16 ICSID Rev.-F.I.L.J. 212 (2002). By contrast, the Most-Favored-Nation Article of this Agreement is expressly limited in its scope to matters "with respect to the establishment, acquisition, expansion, management, conduct, operation, and sale or other disposition of investments." The Parties share the understanding and intent that this clause does not encompass international dispute resolution mechanisms such as those contained in Section C.2.b (Dispute Settlement between a Party and an Investor of Another Party) of this Chapter, and therefore could not reasonably lead to a conclusion similar to that of the Maffezini case."

[212] ICSID Case No. ARB/02/13, Decision on Jurisdiction, 9 November 2004.

[213] Ibid., para. 118.

[214] ICSID Case No. ARB/03/24, Decision on Jurisdiction, 8 February 2005.

[215] ICISD Case No. ARB(AF)/00/2, Award, 29 May 2003.

[216] Ibid., para. 69. This is applied in practice in *ADF Group Inc. v. United States of America*, ICSID Case No. ARB(AF)/00/1, Final Award, 9 January 2003.

[217] ICSID Case ARB/01/7, Award, 25 May 2004, para. 104.

[218] Ibid., para. 104.

[219] This point is developed in *Antoine Goetz v. Republic of Burundi*, ICSID Case No. ARB/95/3, Award, 10 February 1999.

[220] UNCITRAL, First Partial Award, 13 November 2000, paras. 287–288.

[221] ICSID Case No. ARB(AF)/99/1, Award on the Merits, 16 December 2002, para. 103.

[222] UNCITRAL, Interim Award on the Merits, 26 June 2000, para. 102.

[223] ICSID Case No. ARB(AF)/99/1, Award on the Merits, 16 December 2002.

[224] UNCITRAL, Final Award, 3 August 2005, paras. 16–18.

[225] In this regard, see Coe and Rubins 2005, p. 624.

[226] ICSID Case No. ARB(AF)/97/1, Award on the Merits, 16 December 2002.

[227] ICISD Case No. ARB/98/5, Final Award, 26 July 2001.

[228] Ibid., para. 70.

[229] Ibid., para. 73.

[230] ICSID Case No. ARB/96/1, Award on the Merits, 17 February 2000, para. 72.

[231] ICSID Case No. ARB(AF)/00/2, Award, 29 May 2003, para. 121 et seq.

[232] Ibid., para. 116.

[233] See Coe and Rubins 2005, p. 625.

[234] ICSID Case No. ARB(AF)/00/2, Award, 29 May 2003, para. 121.

[235] Among the few BITs containing disciplines on performance requirements are those recently negotiated by Japan, such as the agreements with the Republic of Korea (2002) and Viet Nam (2003). Article 4 of the latter BIT states as follows:

"Article 4

1. *Neither Contracting Party shall impose or enforce, as a condition for investment activities in its Area of an investor of the other Contracting Party, any of the following requirements:*
   - (a) *to export a given level or percentage of goods or services;*
   - (b) *to achieve a given level or percentage of domestic content;*
   - (c) *to purchase, use or accord a preference to goods produced or services provided in its Area, or to purchase goods or services from natural or legal persons or any other entity in its Area;*
   - (d) *o relate the volume or value of imports to the volume or value of exports or to the amount of foreign exchange inflows associated with investments of that investor;*
   - (e) *to restrict sales of goods or services in its Area that investments of that investor produces or provides by relating such sales to the volume or value of its exports or foreign exchange earnings;*
   - (f) *to appoint, as executives, managers or members of boards of directors, individuals of any particular nationality;*
   - (g) *to transfer technology, a production process or other proprietary knowledge to a natural or legal person or any other entity in its Area, except when the requirement (i) is imposed or enforced by a court, administrative tribunal or competition authority to remedy an alleged violation of competition laws; or (ii) concerns the transfer of intellectual property rights which is undertaken in a manner not inconsistent with the Agreement on Trade-Related Aspects of Intellectual Property Rights, Annex 1C of the Marrakesh Agreement Establishing the World Trade Organization;*
   - (h) *to locate the headquarters of that investor for a specific region or the world market in its Area;*
   - (i) *to achieve a given level or value of research and development in its Area; or*
   - (j) *to supply one or more of the goods that the investor produces or the services that the investor provides to a specific region or the world market, exclusively from the Area of the former Contracting Party.*
2. *The provisions of paragraph 1 above do not preclude either Contracting Party from conditioning the receipt or continued receipt of an advantage, in connection with investment activities in its Area of an investor of the other Contracting Party, on compliance with any of the requirements set forth in paragraph 1 (f) through (j) above."*

[236] UNCITRAL, First Partial Award, 13 November 2000, para. 277.

[237] UNCITRAL, Award on Merits, 10 April 2001, para. 80.

[238] ICSID Case No. ARB(AF)/00/1, Final Award, 9 January 2003, para. 173.

III. IMPACT OF INVESTOR-STATE DISPUTE SETTLEMENT EXPERIENCE ON INVESTMENT RULEMAKING

It is evident that the significant increase in the number of ISDS claims over the last decade has had an impact on the process of investment rulemaking. ISDS practice has led numerous countries to realize that the specific wording of IIA provisions does matter, and that it can make a significant difference to the outcome of an investment dispute. Thus, it is no coincidence that several countries in the Asia-Pacific region recently revised their model IIAs and updated their wording, content and structure to incorporate the lessons learned from investment-related litigation experience.

Over the last couple of years, a new generation of IIAs has been gradually emerging. This "new generation" of IIAs falls mainly into two groups. The first group consists of EIAs containing a chapter on investment (UNCTAD 2006a). Originally influenced by NAFTA, such treaties have been concluded relatively frequently, involving countries such as Australia, Canada, Chile, Japan, the Republic of Korea, Malaysia, Mexico, Peru, Thailand and the United States. A second group of IIAs comprising BITs that incorporate important innovations is exemplified by the new model BITs of the United States and Canada.

The normative evolution in these IIAs has five main features:

- First, some recent IIAs have deviated from the traditional open-ended, asset-based definition of investment. Instead, they have attempted to strike a balance between maintaining a comprehensive definition of investment and yet not covering assets that are not intended by the parties to be covered investments.

- Second, the wording of various substantive treaty obligations has been revised. Learning from the technical intricacies faced in the implementation of NAFTA's Chapter 11 and other agreements, new IIAs clarify the meaning of provisions dealing with absolute standards of protection, in particular the international minimum standard of treatment in accordance with international law, and indirect expropriation.

- Third, these IIAs address a broader range of issues – not only specific economic aspects like investment in financial services, but also other kinds of issues where more room for host country regulation is sought. The protection of health, safety, the environment and the promotion of internationally recognized labour rights are areas where new IIAs include specific language aimed at making it clear that the investment promotion and liberalization objectives of IIAs must not be pursued at the expense of these other key public policy goals.

- Fourth, recent IIAs include transparency provisions that represent an important qualitative innovation compared with previous IIAs. Moving from a trend towards conceiving transparency as an obligation to exchange information between countries, these IIAs tend to establish transparency also as an obligation with respect to the investor. Furthermore, transparency obligations are no longer exclusively geared towards fostering exchange of information, but also pertain to transparency in the domestic process of rule-making, aiming to enable interested investors to participate in it.

- Fifth, new IIAs contain significant innovations regarding ISDS procedures. Greater transparency in arbitral proceedings, including open hearings, publication of related legal documents and the possibility for representatives of civil society to submit *amicus curiae* briefs to arbitral tribunals, is foreseen. In addition, other very detailed provisions on ISDS are included in order to provide for more legally oriented, predictable and orderly conduct at the different stages of the ISDS process.

These five innovations are all geared towards providing more certainty regarding the scope and extent of IIA obligations and a more transparent and predictable execution of the ISDS process. Each of these issues is further explained below.

A.   Greater precision in the scope of the definition of investment

Over the last decade, one aspect that generated concern in some countries has been the interpretation by some arbitral tribunals of the concept of "investment" under the applicable IIA. Some of these interpretations were considered to be too broad, and to go beyond what the contracting parties conceived as "investment" when negotiating the IIA. For instance, in *Pope & Talbot v. Canada*[1] the tribunal found that a market share through trade could be regarded as part of the assets of an investment; and in *S.D. Myers v. Canada*[2] the tribunal held that the establishment of a sales office and commitment of marketing time formed a sufficient investment.

Investments can take many forms. This explains why most IIAs use the traditional broad, asset-based definition of investment. The ISDS experience has shown the risks of having an extremely broad and unqualified definition of investment.

One way of avoiding an overreaching definition of investment is to use a "closed-list" definition. This definition differs from the broader asset-based definition in that it does not contain a conceptual chapeau to define the term "investment"; rather, it consists in an ample but finite list of tangible and intangible assets. Originally envisaged as an "enterprise-based" definition used in the context of the United States–Canada Free Trade Agreement, this approach evolved towards the definition used in Article 1139 of NAFTA. Subsequently, the "closed-list" approach has been frequently used by several countries in the definition of "investment" in their IIAs. Article 96 of the Free Trade Agreement (FTA) between Japan and Mexico illustrates this approach by defining "investment" in the following manner:

"(i) the term "investment" means:
   (AA) an enterprise;
   (BB) an equity security of an enterprise;
   (CC) a debt security of an enterprise:
       (aa) where the enterprise is an affiliate of the investor, or
       (bb) where the original maturity of the debt security is at least 3 years, but does not include a debt security, regardless of original maturity, of a Party or a state enterprise;
   (DD) a loan to an enterprise:
       (aa) where the enterprise is an affiliate of the investor, or
       (bb) where the original maturity of the loan is at least 3 years, but does not include a loan, regardless of original maturity, to a Party or a state enterprise;
   (EE) an interest in an enterprise that entitles the owner to share in income or profits of the enterprise;
   (FF) an interest in an enterprise that entitles the owner to share in the assets of that enterprise on dissolution, other than a debt security or a loan excluded from subparagraph (CC) or (DD) above;
   (GG) real estate or other property, tangible or intangible, and any related property rights such as lease, liens and pledges, acquired in the expectation or used for the purpose of economic benefit or other business purposes; and
   (HH) interests arising from the commitment of capital or other resources in the Area of a Party to economic activity in such Area, such as under:
       (aa) contracts involving the presence of an investor's property in the Area of the Party, including turnkey or construction contracts, or concessions, or
       (bb) contracts where remuneration depends substantially on the production, revenues or profits of an enterprise;
   but investment does not mean,
   (II)   claims to money that arise solely from:
       (aa) commercial contracts for the sale of goods or services by a national or enterprise in the Area of a Party to an enterprise in the Area of the other Party, or

> *(bb) the extension of credit in connection with a commercial transaction, such as trade financing, other than a loan covered by subparagraph (DD) above; or*
>
> *(JJ) any other claims to money that do not involve the kinds of interests set out in subparagraphs (AA) through (HH) above;"*

During the last decade, the "closed-list" definition of "investment" has also begun to be used in the context of BIT negotiations. In 2004, Canada abandoned the asset-based definition of "investment" in its foreign investment protection and promotion agreements and opted to incorporate into its new Canadian BIT model a relatively detailed "closed-list" definition of "investment". In addition to being finite, the list contains a series of specific clarifications to prevent the application of the agreement to certain kinds of assets that would otherwise fall under the definition of investment.

As the Canadian experience shows, the difficulty with the "closed-list" approach is not how ample the definition of "investment" should be: countries still prefer a comprehensive definition of "investment" in their IIAs. Rather, it seems that the concern relates to the precision of the definition. In addition to maintaining an ample concept of "investment", countries are eager – as Article 96 of the Japan-Mexico FTA shows – to include clarifications and additional language to make the definition of "investment" more precise.

Another approach used to make the definition of "investment" more accurate has been to qualify an otherwise very broad definition. Accordingly, numerous recently negotiated IIAs incorporate a definition of "investment" in economic terms – that is, they cover, in principle, every asset that an investor owns and controls, but add the qualification that such assets must have the "characteristics of an investment". For this purpose, they refer to criteria developed in ICSID practice, such as *"the commitment of capital or other resources, the expectation of gain or profit, or the assumption of risk"*. This approach is complemented by explicit exclusions of several kinds of assets, which are not to fall within the category of covered investments under the agreement. Article 10.1 of the Free Trade Agreement between Chile and the Republic of Korea illustrates that approach,[3] and defines the term "investment" in the following manner:

> *"**investment** means every kind of asset that an investor owns or controls, directly or indirectly, and that has the characteristics of an investment, such as the commitment of capital or other resources, the expectation of gains or profits and the assumption of risk. Forms that an investment may take include, but are not limited to:*
>
> *(a) an enterprise;*
>
> *(b) shares, stocks, and other forms of equity participation in an enterprise;*
>
> *(c) bonds, debentures, loans, and other debt instruments of an enterprise;*
>
> *(d) rights under contracts, including turnkey, construction, management, production, concession or revenue-sharing contracts;*
>
> *(e) claims to money established and maintained in connection with the conduct of commercial activities;*
>
> *(f) intellectual property rights;*
>
> *(g) rights conferred pursuant to domestic law or contract such as concessions, licenses, authorizations and permits, except for those that do not create any rights protected by domestic law; and*
>
> *(h) other tangible or intangible, movable or immovable property, and related property rights, such as leases, mortgages, liens and pledges;*
>
> *but **investment** does not mean,*
>
> *(i) claims to money that arise solely from:*
>
> > *(i) commercial contracts for the sale of goods or services by a national or enterprise in the territory of a Party to an enterprise in the territory of the other Party; or*
> >
> > *(ii) the extension of credit in connection with a commercial transaction, such as trade financing; and*
>
> *(j) an order entered in a judicial or administrative action."*

The wording of this definition indicates that for an asset to be considered a covered investment, a minimum of three conditions must be satisfied. First, it must be owned or controlled by an investor as defined by the agreement; second, it must have the characteristics of an investment; and third, it must not fall within any of the excluded categories.

The definition does not list all the characteristics that an asset must have in order to be considered an investment. However, the definition does include some minimum parameters, namely the commitment of capital, the expectation of gain or profit or the assumption of risk. The inclusion of these criteria within the definition of investment has the effect of excluding *ab initio* certain assets: arguably, this would be the case for real estate or other property, tangible or intangible, not acquired in the expectation or used for the purpose of economic benefit or other business purposes. However, the wording of the definition means that in the case of other kinds of assets, the determination as to whether they fall within the scope of a covered investment has to be undertaken on a case-by-case basis.

B.   Clarification of the meaning of several key obligations

A second trend in investment rulemaking derived from the ISDS experience over the last decade relates to the revision of the wording of various substantive IIA obligations. New IIAs negotiated by a number of countries, for example Australia, Canada, Chile, Mexico, Singapore and the United States, have tended to clarify the meaning of several substantive provisions, in particular those dealing with absolute standards of protection, such as the international minimum standard of treatment and expropriation.

1. International minimum standard of treatment

In the case of the international minimum standard of treatment, new IIAs include a provision that makes it clear that the obligation undertaken by the contracting parties is to grant covered investments treatment *in accordance with customary international law*. According to these IIAs, the latter includes the notions of fair and equitable treatment and full protection and security. The IIAs also define each of these standards.

It is evident that the negotiators of these agreements took into account the issues discussed in recent NAFTA Chapter 11 arbitrations. An example of this is Article 11.5 of the Free Trade Agreement negotiated between Australia and the United States, which reads as follows:

"Article 11.5: Minimum Standard of Treatment 11-1

1. *Each Party shall accord to covered investments treatment in accordance with the customary international law minimum standard of treatment of aliens, including fair and equitable treatment and full protection and security.*
2. *For greater certainty, the concepts of "fair and equitable treatment" and "full protection and security" do not require treatment in addition to or beyond that which is required by that standard, and do not create additional substantive rights. The obligation in paragraph 1 to provide:*
   (a) "fair and equitable treatment" includes the obligation not to deny justice in criminal, civil, or administrative adjudicatory proceedings in accordance with the principle of due process embodied in the principal legal systems of the world; and
   (b) "full protection and security" requires each Party to provide the level of police protection required under customary international law.
3. *A determination that there has been a breach of another provision of this Agreement, or of a separate international agreement, does not establish that there has been a breach of this Article.*

11-1 Article 11.5 shall be interpreted in accordance with Annex 11-A."

This provision is complemented by an annex that clarifies the understanding of the IIA parties regarding the concept of "customary international law", as follows:

"Annex A
Customary International Law

The Parties confirm their shared understanding that "customary international law" generally and as specifically referenced in Article 11.5 and Annex 11.B results from a general and consistent practice of States that they follow from a sense of legal obligation. With regard to Article 11.5, the customary international law minimum standard of treatment of aliens refers to all customary international law principles that protect the economic rights and interests of aliens."

The language of this clause is self-explanatory. This seems to be exactly the intention of the contracting parties, partly as a result of the experience with Article 1105 of NAFTA. The debate regarding the fair and equitable treatment clause in Chapter 11 of NAFTA, and more recently in some BIT disputes, has evidenced the risks of including unqualified language in IIAs. The wording of such a clause could be broad enough to apply to virtually any adverse circumstance involving an investment, thus making the fair and equitable treatment provision among those provisions most likely to be relied upon by an investor in order to bring a claim under the ISDS proceedings.

The inclusion of language clarifying the content and scope of the minimum standard of treatment in new IIAs may be particularly relevant to counterbalance two recent trends in ISDS practice.

First, the clarification concerning the meaning of customary international law included in, for example, Annex A of the Australia–United States FTA is important for providing guidance as to how to interpret the fair and equitable treatment standard properly. Some recent arbitration panels have granted themselves a certain degree of freedom in this respect. Given the evolutionary nature of customary international law, the content of the fair and equitable treatment standard no longer requires bad faith or "outrageous" behaviour on behalf of the host country. By eliminating these requirements, some arbitral decisions had the effect of equating the minimum standard under customary international law with the plain meaning approach to the text. However, it is not self-evident that customary international law has evolved to such a degree.

Second, the clarification in new IIAs that the minimum standard of treatment comprises two different concepts – the fair and equitable standard, and the standard of full protection and security – is useful for counterbalancing some recent arbitral decisions which merged the two standards in one.

2. Expropriation

Expropriation is the other area where recent IIAs have introduced clarifying language. As was explained above (in subsection II.C.5), the lack of clarity concerning the degree of interference with the rights of ownership that is required for an act or series of acts to constitute an indirect expropriation has been one of the most controversial issues during the last decade (UNCTAD 2000).

The number of ISDS cases acknowledging that an indirect expropriation has occurred has been scant. Nonetheless, parts of civil society in some countries have expressed fears that the prospect of investor–State arbitration arising out of alleged regulatory takings could result in a "regulatory chill" on the ground that concern about liability exposure might lead host countries to abstain from the necessary regulation.

Within this context, recent IIAs contain provisions clarifying two specific aspects. First, text has been included in order to make it explicit that the obligations regarding expropriation are intended to reflect the level of protection granted by customary international law. Second, such clarification has been complemented by guidelines and criteria in order to determine whether, in a particular situation, an indirect expropriation has in fact taken place.

In this regard, it is clarified that an adverse effect on the economic value of an investment, as such, does not establish that an indirect expropriation has occurred. It is further stated that, except in rare circumstances, non-discriminatory regulatory actions by a party aimed at protecting legitimate public welfare objectives, such as public health, safety and the environment, do not constitute indirect expropriations. Annex 10-D of the Free Trade Agreement between Chile and the United States illustrates this trend:

"Annex 10-D
Expropriation

The Parties confirm their shared understanding that:
1. *Article 10.9(1) is intended to reflect customary international law concerning the obligation of States with respect to expropriation.*
2. *An action or a series of actions by a Party cannot constitute an expropriation unless it interferes with a tangible or intangible property right or property interest in an investment.*
3. *Article 10.9(1) addresses two situations. The first is direct expropriation, where an investment is nationalized or otherwise directly expropriated through formal transfer of title or outright seizure.*
4. *The second situation addressed by Article 10.9(1) is indirect expropriation, where an action or series of actions by a Party has an effect equivalent to direct expropriation without formal transfer of title or outright seizure.*
   (a) *The determination of whether an action or series of actions by a Party, in a specific fact situation, constitutes an indirect expropriation, requires a case-by- case, fact-based inquiry that considers, among other factors:*
      (i) *the economic impact of the government action, although the fact that an action or series of actions by a Party has an adverse effect on the economic value of an investment, standing alone, does not establish that an indirect expropriation has occurred;*
      (ii) *the extent to which the government action interferes with distinct, reasonable investment-backed expectations; and*
      (iii) *the character of the government action.*
   (b) *Except in rare circumstances, nondiscriminatory regulatory actions by a Party that are designed and applied to protect legitimate public welfare objectives, such as public health, safety, and the environment, do not constitute indirect expropriations."*

What are the reasons for the inclusion of these clarification clauses in some IIAs? Do these clauses reflect the intention of the contracting parties to "correct" any particular trend in the jurisprudential interpretation of expropriation clauses? It could be argued that such provisions provide some important guidance for future cases. Another significant role of clarifying provisions may be that of serving as a signal for civil society. By including such language, Governments may acknowledge the concerns of certain sectors of civil society regarding what they perceive as a "regulatory chill effect" of ISDS proceedings. To respond to these concerns, a provision such as the one cited above indicates that IIAs are not intended to call in question the regulatory power of host countries.

C.   Clarification that investment protection should not be pursued at the expense of other public policy objectives: Non-lowering-of-standards clause

In addition to the features already mentioned, some new IIAs address a broader scope of issues. The protection of health, safety, cultural identity, the environment and the promotion of internationally recognized labour rights are some of the areas where these IIAs include specific language aimed at making clear that the investment promotion and liberalization objectives of IIAs must not be pursued at the expense of these other key public policy objectives. Different techniques have been used for that purpose. While some IIAs have included general treaty exceptions, others have opted for positive language in order to reinforce contracting parties' commitments to safeguard certain values; some IIAs have combined exceptions and positive language.

Examples of IIAs including exceptions to safeguard flexibility for regulations are the new United States and Canadian model BITs. The latter includes a series of exceptions to preserve a wide range of public policy objectives, such as the protection of human, animal or plant life and health, the integrity and stability of the financial system, cultural industries and essential security interest, although on a best-efforts and non-binding basis only. For example, the 2004 Canadian model BIT includes the following provision:

"Article 11
Health, Safety and Environmental Measures

The Parties recognize that it is inappropriate to encourage investment by relaxing domestic health, safety or environmental measures. Accordingly, a Party should not waive or otherwise derogate from, or offer to waive or otherwise derogate from, such measures as an encouragement for the establishment, acquisition, expansion or retention in its territory or an investment of an investor. If a Party considers that the other Party has offered such an encouragement, it may request consultations with the other Party and the two Parties shall consult with a view to avoiding any such encouragement."[4]

Countries have not only opted to use exceptions, but also included positive language in IIAs to protect other public policy objectives, notably protection of the environment and respect for core labour rights. Once more, the legal techniques used for that purpose vary among the different IIAs. One approach has been to make reference to these values in the preamble of the agreement. For instance, the BIT between Japan and Viet Nam (2003) explicitly provides in its preamble that the objective to promote investment can be achieved *"without relaxing health, safety and environmental measures of general application"*.

Other IIAs have included "side agreements" to protect labour and environmental standards. For instance, in the context of the Trans-Pacific Strategic Economic Partnership Agreement between Brunei Darussalam, Chile, New Zealand and Singapore (2005),[5] the contracting parties negotiated two side agreements, on environment[6] and labour cooperation[7] respectively. It is made clear, inter alia, that investment promotion and liberalization will not impair the ability of the contracting parties to protect the environment or labour rights in their respective territories. The same technique can be observed in NAFTA and in the Free Trade Agreement between Canada and Chile (1996).

Other IIAs have incorporated specific provisions into the investment chapter as well as into additional sections on labour and environment. This is the case of several free trade agreements negotiated by the United States with countries such as Australia (2004), Chile (2003), Singapore (2003) and Peru (2006). The investment chapters in these IIAs include a provision similar to Article 10.18 of the Free Trade Agreement between Chile and the Republic of Korea (2003), which states as follows:

"Article 10.18: Environmental Measures

1. Nothing in this Chapter shall be construed to prevent a Party from adopting, maintaining or enforcing any measure otherwise consistent with this Chapter that it considers appropriate to ensure that an investment activity in its territory is undertaken in a manner sensitive to environmental concerns.

2. The Parties recognize that it is inappropriate to encourage investment by relaxing domestic health, safety or environmental measures. Accordingly, a Party should not waive or otherwise derogate from, or offer to waive or otherwise derogate from, such measures as an encouragement for the establishment, acquisition, expansion or retention in its territory of an investment of an investor. If a Party considers that the other Party has offered such an encouragement, it may request consultations with the other Party and the Parties shall consult with a view to avoiding any such encouragement."

The inclusion of language providing that the protection and liberalization of investment should not be pursued at the expense of other key public policy objectives may be more an indirect than a direct result of ISDS practice over the last decade. These normative developments seem to be in keeping with the intention of the contracting parties to address the concerns of labour unions and environmental NGOs regarding investment agreements.

D.   Promotion of greater transparency between the contracting parties and in the process of domestic rule-making

A fourth feature of some recent IIAs is the qualitative evolution in the conception of the transparency obligations for the purposes of the agreement. In addition to the obligation of the contracting parties to publish their laws,[8] new approaches include the investors in transparency regulations, giving them not only rights, but also obligations vis-à-vis the host country.[9] Second, this new method conceives transparency beyond the traditional notion of publication of laws and regulations. Rather, it also focuses on the process of rulemaking, attempting to use it as an instrument to promote the principle of due process. Thus, in addition to enabling investors to know and understand the applicable rules and disciplines affecting their investments, this new approach attempts to use transparency as a tool to enable interested persons to participate in the process of investment-related rulemaking. An example of this approach is Article 19 of the 2004 Canadian model BIT:

"Article 19
Transparency

1. *Each Party shall, to the extent possible, ensure that its laws, regulations, procedures, and administrative rulings of general application respecting any matter covered by this Agreement are promptly published or otherwise made available in such a manner as to enable interested persons and the other Party to become acquainted with them.*
2. *To the extent possible, each Party shall:*
    (a) publish in advance any such measure that it proposes to adopt; and
    (b) provide interested persons and the other Party a reasonable opportunity to comment on such proposed measures.
3. *Upon request by a Party, information shall be exchanged on the measures of the other Party that may have an impact on covered investments."*

This approach applies transparency not only to existing legislation, but also to draft laws and regulations. In this respect, Article 19.2 above provides that to the extent possible the Contracting Parties shall publish in advance any proposed measure of general application that affects investments, and also "[…] *provide interested persons and the other Party a reasonable opportunity to comment on such proposed measures*". This approach, which is also used in the new United States model BIT, represents a qualitative leap in the content and rationale of transparency provisions in IIAs. Several factors bear out that statement.

First, under this approach, transparency no longer means just information, but also participation in investment rulemaking. Second, the obligation does not provide an exclusive right to a foreign investor vis-à-vis the host country. Rather, the obligation is to provide a reasonable opportunity to all interested persons to comment on proposed investment-related measures. Thus, the obligation is applicable not only to the contracting parties with respect to the investors of the other contracting party, but also between each contracting party and its own citizens.

For some countries, to develop the mechanisms to effectively comply with the principles of due process may entail legal reforms and financial costs. On the other hand, if those adjustments are necessary it is because the countries concerned lack a modern body of administrative law and implementation procedures, which is a prerequisite not only for the modernization of the administration of justice, but also for strengthening democratic institutions in general. Within this context, transparency provisions in IIAs may be seen not only to play a significant role for the generation of a more predictable business climate in favour of foreign investors, but also – and more important from a development perspective – to foster a more legalistic and rule-oriented administrative practice, which is in the general interest of the population of the host country.

The emphasis by some IIAs on using transparency provisions to strengthen the principle of due process of law is also evidenced by a number of additional obligations. An example is the BIT between the United States and Uruguay (2005), which includes within the transparency provision additional explicit obligations regarding administrative procedures and the right to an impartial review and appeal of administrative decisions on investment-related matters. Once more, these kinds of obligations matter not only because of the more predictable investment climate they tend to generate, but also because of the institutional strengthening that their full compliance may entail for the citizens of the countries concerned.

E.   Innovations in ISDS procedures

Some recent IIAs regulate in more detail ISDS procedures, providing greater guidance, both to the disputing parties and to tribunals, with respect to the conduct of the arbitration proceedings. During the first part of the last decade, Chapter 11 of NAFTA had a significant influence on the features of ISDS provisions in many other IIAs. More recently, it is the experience with the increasing number of investment disputes that has triggered innovations in new IIAs.

Traditionally, most IIAs have had very few general provisions on ISDS procedures. This trend changed with NAFTA, which for the first time regulated a series of aspects of arbitration proceedings. NAFTA's Chapter 11 devotes a whole section to ISDS procedures. Recent IIAs have continued with this trend, and have even taken the evolution in rule-making one step further. Indeed, ISDS procedures are one of the areas where there have been significant developments in IIAs over the last decade.

Recent IIAs have incorporated various innovative provisions to achieve four general objectives: to provide greater control by the contracting parties over arbitration procedures; second, to promote the principle of judicial economy in investment-related disputes; third, to ensure consistency among arbitral awards; and fourth, to promote greater legitimacy of ISDS within civil society. These objectives are derived from the experience with investment disputes that several countries in the region have gathered over the last decade. Each one is examined in greater detail below.

1.   Greater control by the contracting parties over arbitration procedures

Some recent IIAs contain innovations geared towards promoting greater control by the contracting parties over arbitration procedures. The purpose is to reduce the degree of discretion that arbitral tribunals have in deciding how to conduct the arbitration proceedings, and thus to make the latter more predictable, in addition to clarifying key substantive treaty provisions. Two different techniques have been used to pursue this objective.

First, several countries have opted to increase the level of detail of procedural aspects of ISDS in order to clarify in advance certain issues that otherwise would have to be decided by arbitral tribunals. New IIAs draw from the experience of NAFTA, and contain more detailed ISDS provisions. Examples include the specific procedures applicable when submitting a notice of intent for arbitration, provisions to prevent the same dispute from being simultaneously addressed in more than one legal forum, specific procedures for the appointment of arbitrators and expert review groups, specification of the place of arbitration, measures for interim injunctive relief, preliminary objections, conduct of arbitral proceedings and enforcement of awards. Some recent IIAs even go beyond NAFTA and contain clauses that clarify particular procedural aspects that have been the subject of debate in ISDS practice over the last decade.

For instance, the investment chapter in the free trade agreement between Singapore and the United States explicitly addresses one of the issues that have been discussed in the context of the application of other IIAs – namely, whether treaty-based arbitral tribunals have jurisdiction to deal with claims based solely on an investment contract. In this regard, the agreement between Singapore and the United States expressly provides in its Article 15.15 that an investor can submit a claim under that IIA on the basis of a breach of an investment agreement or an investment authorization:

"Article 15.15: Submission of a Claim to Arbitration

1. In the event that a disputing party considers that an investment dispute cannot be settled by consultation and negotiation:
   (a) the claimant, on its own behalf, may submit to arbitration under this Section a claim:
      (i) that the respondent has breached
         (A) an obligation under Section B,
         (B) an investment authorization, or
         (C) an investment agreement; and
      (ii) that the claimant has incurred loss or damage by reason of, or arising out of, that breach; and
   (b) the claimant, on behalf of an enterprise of the respondent that is a juridical person that the claimant owns or controls directly or indirectly, may submit to arbitration under this Section a claim:
      (i) that the respondent has breached
         (A) an obligation under Section B,
         (B) an investment authorization, or
         (C) an investment agreement; and
      (ii) that the enterprise has incurred loss or damage by reason of, or arising out of, that breach. [...]."

Similar provisions have been included in other recent IIAs.[10] This greater involvement of the contracting parties in shaping the specific features of ISDS mechanisms demonstrates their interest in increasing the predictability of arbitration procedures and control over their execution.

A second means by which contracting parties have sought to increase their control over the arbitration proceedings arises at the stage of implementation of these mechanisms. Several recent IIAs have included provisions ensuring the involvement of the contracting parties in arbitration proceedings that address specific subject matters, such as financial services, the interpretation of non-conforming measures or taxation measures. In all these cases, these IIAs contain provisions that grant specialized competent authorities of the contracting parties the right to make interpretations of certain matters or provisions of the agreement, which will be binding for the arbitral tribunal.

For example, Article 10.36 of the investment chapter of the free trade agreement between the Chile and the Republic of Korea provides that when a respondent invokes a non-conforming measure as a defence to a claim, it will be in principle the Commission (composed of ministers of both contracting parties), and not the arbitral tribunal, that will interpret the non-conforming measure. That provision reads as follows:

"Article 10.36: Interpretation of Annexes

1. *Where a disputing Party asserts as a defence that the measure alleged to be a breach is within the scope of a reservation or exception set out in Annex I or Annex II, upon request of the disputing Party, the Tribunal shall request the interpretation of the Commission on the issue. The Commission, within 60 days of delivery of the request, shall submit in writing its interpretation to the Tribunal.*

2. *Further to paragraph 2 of Article 10.35, a Commission interpretation submitted under paragraph 1 shall be binding on the Tribunal. If the Commission fails to submit an interpretation within 60 days, the Tribunal shall decide the issue."*

Another example of this trend is Article 17, paragraphs 1 and 2, of the 2004 Canadian model BIT. It provides that where an investor submits a claim to arbitration related to financial services, and the disputing contracting party, as a defence, invokes the general exception based on prudential reasons in Articles 10(2) or 14(6) of the agreement, the arbitral tribunal

"[…] shall, at the request of that Party, seek a report in writing from the Parties on the issue of whether and to what extent the said paragraphs are a valid defence to the claim of the investor. The tribunal may not proceed pending receipt of a report under this Article […] The Parties shall proceed […] to prepare a written report, either on the basis of agreement following consultations, or by means of an arbitral panel. The consultations shall be between the financial services authorities of the Parties. The report shall be transmitted to the Tribunal, and shall be binding on the Tribunal."

Rather than relying on the judgement of the arbitral tribunal, the mechanism cited above aims to reserve for the competent authorities of the contracting parties – at least in the first instance – the right to decide whether a claim brought by an investor should be discarded on the grounds of a general exception based on prudential reasons.

In sum, the two examples cited above evidence a pattern in new IIAs – the intention of the contracting parties to enhance their control over the interpretation of certain key provisions of the agreements. The underlying assumption is that the contracting parties are better suited than an arbitral tribunal to assess certain specific matters, for example the interpretation of non-conforming measures or prudential measures for financial services.

2. Promotion of judicial economy

To properly defend a case in ISDS proceedings entails a significant amount of time and resources for the parties involved in the dispute. Therefore, some countries recently agreed to include various procedural innovations in their IIAs that may be instrumental in fostering the principle of judicial economy in ISDS procedures.

Three particular mechanisms illustrate this trend. One is a specific provision dealing with potential "frivolous claims" submitted by an investor. Another element is the possibility of consolidating separate claims that have a question of law or fact in common, and arise out of the same events or circumstances. The third mechanism fostering judicial economy prevents a particular investment dispute from being addressed in more than one adjudication forum at the same time. While the first of these mechanisms represents an innovation in recent IIAs, the other two mechanisms were originally included in NAFTA and have become a common feature among new IIAs. Each of these mechanisms is explained below in more detail.

a. Mechanism to avoid "frivolous claims"

The significant increase in investment disputes over the last decade has given rise to the concern that investors may abuse the system. Investors may be eager to claim as many violations of the applicable IIA as possible in order to increase their chances of success. This may take a heavy toll in terms of time, effort, fees and other costs, not only for the parties to the dispute, but also for the arbitral tribunal.

It is within this context that several countries have advocated a procedure to avoid "frivolous claims" in investment-related disputes, namely claims that evidently lack a sound legal basis. Thus, several recent IIAs include a provision that makes it possible for the arbitral tribunal to apply an "admissibility test" to the claims submitted. In accordance with this provision, a tribunal can address and decide as a preliminary question any objection raised by the respondent that, as a matter of law, a claim submitted is not a claim for which an award in favour of the claimant may be rendered. In deciding upon an objection under this procedure, the arbitration tribunal will assume that the claimant's factual allegations in support of the claims are true, and will issue a decision or award on the objection on an expedited basis.

The experience of the dispute in *Methanex v. United States* had an important influence on this particular innovation in investment rulemaking. In that case, the tribunal addressed the distinction between the concept of admissibility and the concept of jurisdiction.[11]

The United States challenged the admissibility of Methanex's claims on the basis that – even assuming that all the facts alleged by Methanex were true – there could never be a breach of the substantive obligation provisions pleaded by the claimant. Hence, according to the United States, Methanex's claims were bound to fail. The tribunal found that the UNCITRAL Arbitration Rules do not grant arbitral tribunals the authority to reject claims on the ground that they are not admissible.[12] Consequently, the tribunal concluded that it had no express or implied power to reject claims on the basis of this type of objection to admissibility.

The introduction of a specific provision empowering arbitral tribunals to reject the admissibility of claims lacking a legal basis is thus one of the significant innovations of new IIAs. Article 10.19, paragraphs 4 and 5, of the investment chapter of the free trade agreement between the United States and Chile illustrates that approach:[13]

"Article 10.19 Conduct of the Arbitration

[…]

4. *Without prejudice to a tribunal's authority to address other objections as a preliminary question, such as an objection that a dispute is not within a tribunal's competence, a tribunal shall address and decide as a preliminary question any objection by the respondent that, as a matter of law, a claim submitted is not a claim for which an award in favor of the claimant may be made under Article 10.25.*

    (a) *Such objection shall be submitted to the tribunal as soon as possible after the tribunal is constituted, and in no event later than the date the tribunal fixes for the respondent to submit its counter-memorial (or, in the case of an amendment to the notice of arbitration referred to in Article 10.15(6), the date the tribunal fixes for the respondent to submit its response to the amendment).*

    (b) *On receipt of an objection under this paragraph, the tribunal shall suspend any proceedings on the merits, establish a schedule for considering the objection consistent with any schedule it has established for considering any other preliminary question, and issue a decision or award on the objection, stating the grounds therefore.*

    (c) *In deciding an objection under this paragraph, the tribunal shall assume to be true claimant's factual allegations in support of any claim in the notice of arbitration (or any amendment thereof) and, in disputes brought under the UNCITRAL Arbitration Rules, the statement of claim referred to in Article 18 of the UNCITRAL Arbitration Rules. The tribunal may also consider any relevant facts not in dispute.*

(d) The respondent does not waive any objection as to competence or any argument on the merits merely because the respondent did or did not raise an objection under this paragraph or make use of the expedited procedure set out in the following paragraph.

5. In the event that the respondent so requests within 45 days after the tribunal is constituted, the tribunal shall decide on an expedited basis an objection under paragraph 4 or any objection that the dispute is not within the tribunal's competence. The tribunal shall suspend any proceedings on the merits and issue a decision or award on the objection(s), stating the grounds therefore, no later than 150 days after the date of the request. However, if a disputing party requests a hearing, the tribunal may take an additional 30 days to issue the decision or award. Regardless of whether a hearing is requested, a tribunal may, on a showing of extraordinary cause, delay issuing its decision or award by an additional brief period of time, which may not exceed 30 days.

6. When it decides a respondent's objection under paragraph 4 or 5, the tribunal may, if warranted, award to the prevailing disputing party reasonable costs and attorneys' fees incurred in submitting or opposing the objection. In determining whether such an award is warranted, the tribunal shall consider whether either the claimant's claim or the respondent's objection was frivolous, and shall provide the disputing parties a reasonable opportunity to comment."

The objective of the expedited procedure in that provision is to enable arbitral tribunals to reject a claim as inadmissible, and thus avoid spending time and resources on adjudicating a dispute generated by claims that lack any sound legal foundation. Furthermore, the contracting parties' intention to promote judicial economy is evidenced by the specific time frames provided in paragraph 5 of Article 10.19 above. It should be noted that under this provision, not all claims that are inadmissible are necessarily frivolous. Such a determination will be for the tribunal to make. Presumably, where a claim is found to be frivolous, this determination will have an impact on the award concerning costs and lawyers' fees.

b. Consolidation of claims

Another mechanism included in recent IIAs in order to foster judicial economy – as well as to reduce the risk of inconsistent results – is a provision allowing the consolidation of separate claims that have a question of law or fact in common, and arise out of the same events or circumstances. Most IIAs concluded by Mexico during the last decade, as well as the IIAs recently negotiated by the United States and the 2004 Canadian model BIT, include provisions that authorize the formation of a special tribunal to assume jurisdiction over separate claims that have a question of law or fact in common. Article 83 of the investment chapter of the FTA between Mexico and Japan (2004) illustrates that approach:

"Article 83
Consolidation of Multiple Claims

1. When a disputing party considers that two or more claims submitted to arbitration [...] have a question of law or fact in common, the disputing party may seek a consolidation order in accordance with the terms of paragraphs 2 through 9 below.
[...]
4. A Tribunal established under this Article shall be established under the ICSID Convention or the ICSID Additional Facility Rules as may be amended, as appropriate, and shall conduct its proceedings in accordance with the provisions thereof, except as modified by this Section.

[...]

8. *A Tribunal established under this Article may, in the interests of fair and efficient resolution of the dispute, and after hearing the disputing parties, by order:*

   (a) *assume jurisdiction over, and hear and determine together, all or part of the claims* [...] *or*

   (b) *assume jurisdiction over, and hear and determine one or more of the claims* [...] *the determination of which it believes would assist in the resolution of the others.* [...]"

When two or more claims arising out of the same legal or factual matters are consolidated in a single arbitral proceeding, judicial economy is promoted and there is no risk that a contracting party will simultaneously face several disputes as a result of multiple challenges against the same contested measure.

c. Mechanism to prevent a dispute from being submitted to more than one dispute settlement forum: Improving the "fork in the road"

The increase in the number of investment disputes demonstrates the importance of preventing a particular investment dispute from being addressed in more than one dispute settlement forum at the same time. If that is not done, the host country will be required to respond to the same claims more than once and there will thus be the risk of inconsistent decisions. Of special concern is the possibility of the investor's submitting a dispute to the domestic courts of the host country and simultaneously or subsequently to international arbitration. The purpose of "fork-in-the-road" provisions is to exclude that possibility. However, ISDS practice over the last decade has shown that their ability to achieve that purpose is somewhat deficient.

As explained above (in subsection II.B.1.e), it has been found in ISDS practice that *litis pendens* exists only where there is an identity of *parties, object and cause of action*. Thus, arbitral awards have interpreted the "fork-in-the-road" provision as resulting in a loss of access to international arbitration only where the dispute and the parties before the domestic courts are identical with the dispute and the parties in the international proceeding. This interpretation has made "fork-in-the-road" provisions very difficult to invoke. For instance, it is easy to envisage a situation in which a shareholder initiates an arbitration to protect its rights under the IIA, while the investment (i.e. the subsidiary) initiates a domestic dispute to protect its contract or other legal rights, including those derived from the IIA.[14]

Most IIAs negotiated recently do not use "fork-in-the-road" clauses. Instead, they use a different approach to achieve the same objective in a more effective manner. This approach is known in the investment literature as the "no-U-turn", and focuses on the measure that has triggered the dispute. It makes it possible for the investor to decide the venue for the resolution of the dispute even after the investor has submitted it to the administrative or judicial tribunals of the host country. The "no-U-turn" concept allows the investor to opt for international arbitration as long as domestic tribunals have not rendered a final judgement on the dispute. Article XIII.3 of the BIT between Canada and Thailand (1997) illustrates this approach, and provides that an investor may submit a dispute to arbitration only if

"[…] *the investor has waived to initiate or continue any other proceedings in relation to the measure that is alleged to be in breach of this Agreement before the courts or tribunals of the Contracting Party concerned or in a dispute settlement procedure of any kind.*"

This approach also forecloses another situation in which the same dispute could be submitted to multiple forums. This would be the case if an investor first submitted the dispute to arbitration, and – depending on the outcome – then decided to submit it to local courts. Such a result would be prevented under the clause cited above, since, prior to submitting the claim to international arbitration, the investor would have to waive the right to continue or initiate any other proceeding before the national courts of the contracting party concerned or in any other forum.

3. Promotion of a consistent and sound jurisprudence on international investment law

A third category of innovation in investor–State arbitration provisions in IIAs is geared towards ensuring a consistent and correct application of international law in arbitral awards. As previously explained, recent IIAs have been negotiated in the context of a significant increase in investor–State disputes. These disputes have resulted in awards that have not always been consistent, and, in some cases, have rendered controversial legal interpretations of the terms of the investment agreements and of international law in general. Some recent IIAs have included innovative provisions to foster a consistent and sound development of jurisprudence. This objective has been pursued mainly through in two different ways.

One way has been to include in IIAs more detailed provisions on several key substantive issues, the interpretation of which has been controversial in arbitration proceedings. For example, the United States and Canada have recently modified the language of their IIAs to clarify the content of the fair and equitable treatment standard and the concept of indirect expropriation. The intention was to limit the scope that arbitral tribunals might otherwise give to the relevant IIA provisions.

Another method, aimed at preventing incorrect or inconsistent jurisprudence, has been the proposal that arbitral awards be subject to appeal. For example, the investment chapter of the free trade agreement between Peru and the United States provides that within three years of the entry into force of the agreement, the parties shall consider whether to establish an appellate body to review awards. In particular, Annex 10-D provides as follows:

> "*Annex 10-D*
> *Possibility of a Bilateral Appellate Body/Mechanism*
>
> *Within three years after the date of entry into force of this Agreement, the Parties shall consider whether to establish an appellate body or similar mechanism to review awards rendered under Article 10.26 in arbitrations commenced after they establish the appellate body or similar mechanism.*"

The potential establishment of appellate mechanisms raises many issues that require in-depth discussion. There is currently no clarity regarding the particular features of such mechanisms and its interaction with the existing arbitration conventions or IIAs negotiated by the parties concerned. Furthermore, if the main purpose of an appellate mechanism is to ensure consistency in arbitral awards and in the development of international investment law, it should bring under its umbrella most – if not all – existing IIAs. This could not be done by an appellate mechanism established by a single BIT or several such treaties.

4. Promotion of the legitimacy of investor–State arbitration within civil society

There is a fourth category of innovations that has emerged in recently negotiated IIAs. They are geared towards improving the legitimacy of investor–State arbitration within civil society. Some new IIAs have added provisions intended to respond to concerns that have arisen over the years among some civil society organizations with respect to investor–State dispute resolution. One such concern relates to the limited transparency of dispute resolution proceedings. In response to those concerns, the 2004 Canadian model BIT and the IIAs recently negotiated by the United States include provisions to promote the transparency of arbitration proceedings.

For instance, the IIAs negotiated between the United States, on the one hand, and Chile, Peru, and Singapore, on the other hand, require the respondent in an investment dispute to transmit to the home country and to make available to the public certain documents, including the notice of arbitration, the memorials, the transcripts of hearings and the awards of the tribunal. Transparency provisions in these IIAs also require that the hearings be open to the public, although there are provisions to protect confidential business information. However, the provisions do not require the parties to make public any settlement discussions, nor do they   with the confidentiality of the tribunal's deliberations.

The trend towards fostering transparency in ISDS procedures goes beyond allowing the public to be informed about the different stages of the arbitral proceedings. Several new IIAs, such as the 2004 Canadian model BIT and IIAs negotiated by the United States, also allow parties not involved in the dispute to submit briefs, and authorize arbitral tribunals to consider submissions from any member of civil society. As a result of allowing civil society to participate in arbitral proceedings, contracting parties had to regulate in detail the procedures under which *amicus curiae* briefs were to be submitted and handled, endeavouring to prevent these submissions from negatively affecting the conduct of the arbitration. This explains, for instance, the screening mechanism in Article 39 of the 2004 Canadian model BIT. It first establishes certain criteria under which the arbitral tribunal would decide whether a non-disputing party may file a submission, and – if authorization is given – provides guidance to the tribunal as to the weight that the submission should have in the proceedings. In its relevant parts, Article 39 provides as follows:

"Article 39
Submissions by a Non-Disputing Party

1. *Any non-disputing party that is a person of a Party, or has a significant presence in the territory of a Party, that wishes to file a written submission with a Tribunal (the "applicant") shall apply for leave from the Tribunal to file such a submission. […]*
2. *The applicant shall serve the application for leave to file a non-disputing party submission and the submission on all disputing parties and the Tribunal.*
3. *The Tribunal shall set an appropriate date for the disputing parties to comment on the application for leave to file a non-disputing party submission.*
4. *In determining whether to grant leave to file a non-disputing party submission, the Tribunal shall consider, among other things, the extent to which:*
   (a) *the non-disputing party submission would assist the Tribunal in the determination of a factual or legal issue related to the arbitration by bringing a perspective, particular knowledge or insight that is different from that of the disputing parties;*
   (b) *the non-disputing party submission would address a matter within the scope of the dispute;*
   (c) *the non-disputing party has a significant interest in the arbitration; and*
   (d) *there is a public interest in the subject-matter of the arbitration.*
5. *The Tribunal shall ensure that:*
   (a) *any non-disputing party submission does not disrupt the proceedings; and*
   (b) *neither disputing party is unduly burdened or unfairly prejudiced by such submissions.*
6. *The Tribunal shall decide whether to grant leave to file a non-disputing party submission. If leave to file a non-disputing party submission is granted, the Tribunal shall set an appropriate date for the disputing parties to respond in writing to the non-disputing party submission. By that date, the non-disputing Party may, pursuant to Article 34 (Participation by the Non-Disputing Party), address any issues of interpretation of this Agreement presented in the non-disputing party submission.*
7. *The Tribunal that grants leave to file a non-disputing party submission is not required to address the submission at any point in the arbitration, nor is the non-disputing party that files the submission entitled to make further submissions in the arbitration. […]"*

This approach demonstrates that transparency provisions serve important goals; however, they may also increase the burden on the parties to the dispute and limit their discretion. For example, parties may feel the need to submit additional materials responding to arguments made in the *amicus curiae* briefs. Public knowledge of the disputes may result in public pressure on the parties to settle or to refuse to settle certain disputes. Such pressure may undermine one of the main objectives of ISDS procedures, namely to foster a rule-oriented adjudication mechanism, where politics interfere as little as possible with the development of a sound international legal investment regime.

F.   Promotion of investment protection and gradual liberalization of investment

The previous sections have explained how the international experience with investment disputes has had an impact on investment rulemaking. *New generation* IIAs have become more sophisticated, attempting to define "investment" more precisely, clarifying certain key standards of protection, specifying in greater detail ISDS procedures and promoting a balance between investment protection and liberalization and other key public policy objectives. Despite the challenges generated by an increase in litigation activity, new generation IIAs have not lost their main rationale, which is to promote investment protection and the gradual liberalization of investment flows.

International investment rules have increasingly been adopted as part of bilateral, regional, interregional and plurilateral preferential agreements that address, and seek to facilitate, trade and investment transactions. Indeed, investment rules are increasingly being formulated as part of agreements that encompass a broader set of issues, including in particular trade in goods and services, and other production factors. These agreements, in addition to containing a variable range of trade liberalization and promotion provisions, contain commitments to liberalize, protect and/or promote investment flows between the parties. As explained above (in subsection I.A), the number of such agreements has been growing steadily over the last decade, with more than 87 per cent having been concluded since the 1990s.

Some new IIAs – both BITs and economic integration agreements (EIAs) – provide not only for investment protection but also for gradual liberalization. That is the case of IIAs concluded by countries such as Canada, Chile, Japan, Mexico, Peru, Singapore and the United States. These IIAs are more comprehensive, detailed and, for the most part, more rigorous than any agreements previously concluded. While they address many of the same topics, they also deal with additional issues or modify the approach taken in NAFTA on the basis of accumulated experience.

These IIAs grant to covered foreign investors national treatment and MFN treatment with respect to the right of establishment in the host country. This right is generally qualified by a provision that allows the host country to specify sectors or activities of the economy in which the right does not apply, the so-called negative list approach. This approach was pioneered by the United States in its BITs, but in recent years has also been used by Canada and Japan in their BITs, and by various other countries in their EIAs.

As more agreements utilizing this approach are being concluded, the annexes have also become somewhat more complex. For example, some agreements concluded in recent years include separate annexes. One annex includes a list of existing laws and regulations that are inconsistent with one or several of the obligations and in respect of which contracting parties may enter reservations. The effect of an annex of non-conforming measures is to bind the level of conformity existing between the domestic legislation of the contracting parties and the obligations of the IIA at the time of conclusion of the agreement. Thus, once the IIA enters into force, parties may amend any of the non-conforming measures included in the annex only if the amendment does not diminish the conformity of the measure with the obligation concerned, as it existed immediately before the amendment. Article 6 the BIT negotiated between Japan and Viet Nam (2003) illustrates that approach:

"Article 6

1. *Notwithstanding the provisions of Article 2 or 4, each Contracting Party may maintain any exceptional measure, which exists on the date on which this Agreement comes into force, in the sectors or with respect to the matters specified in Annex II to this Agreement.*

2. *Each Contracting Party shall, on the date on which this Agreement comes into force, notify the other Contracting Party of all existing exceptional measures in the sectors or*

with respect to the matters specified in Annex II. Such notification shall include information on the following elements of each exceptional measure: (a) sector and sub-sector or matter; (b) obligation or article in respect of the exceptional measure; (c) legal source of the exceptional measure; (d) succinct description of the exceptional measure; and (e) purpose of the exceptional measure.

3. *Each Contracting Party shall endeavour to progressively reduce or eliminate the exceptional measures notified pursuant to paragraph 2 above.*

4. *Neither Contracting Party shall, after the entry into force of this Agreement, adopt any new exceptional measure in the sectors or with respect to the matters specified in Annex II."*

Most of these IIAs also envisage a second kind of annex, which comprises a list of economic activities or sectors where the contracting parties may maintain or adopt measures inconsistent with one or several of the obligations of the IIA. Thus, in the areas or sectors included in this second annex, parties do not enter into binding commitments. Instead, the contracting parties reserve their right to adopt new non-conforming measures that may have not existed at the time of negotiations. This is why this kind of annex is often known as the annex of "future measures". For example, Article 10.9 of the investment chapter of the FTA between Chile and the Republic of Korea states as follows:

"Article 10.9: Reservations and Exceptions
[...]
2. Articles 10.3 [national treatment]*, 10.7* [Performance Requirements] *and 10.8* [Senior Management and Boards of Directors] *shall not apply to any measure that a Party adopts or maintains with respect to sectors, subsectors or activities, as set out in its Schedule to Annex II.* [...]"

The use of the negative list approach, combined with the increased sophistication of the annexes, shows that signatories to new generation IIAs have not experienced any regulatory "chilling effect" resulting from the increase in investment disputes over the last decade. Furthermore, the response of Governments negotiating new generation IIAs has not been to ignore the importance of continuing to promote and protect international investment flows.

Notes

[1] UNCITRAL, Interim Award on Merits, 26 June 2000; Award on Merits, 10 April 2001; Award on Damages, 31 May 2002; Award on Costs, 26 November 2002.

[2] UNCITRAL, First Partial Award, 13 November 2000.

[3] Other agreements using this approach are the free trade agreements recently negotiated between the United States and Australia, Singapore and Chile respectively (chapter on investment).

[4] The new United States model BIT contains similar provisions on investment and environment and investment and labour.

[5] This agreement applies to investment in services only.

[6] Environment Cooperation Agreement among the Parties to the Trans-Pacific Strategic Economic Partnership Agreement.

[7] Memorandum of Understanding on Labour Cooperation among the Parties to the Trans-Pacific Strategic Economic Partnership Agreement.

[8] For instance, Article10 of the BIT between Uruguay and the United States (2005) provides as follows:
   "*Article 10: Publication of Laws and Decisions Respecting Investment*
   1. Each Party shall ensure that its:
   (a) laws, regulations, procedures, and administrative rulings of general application; and
   (b) adjudicatory decisions respecting any matter covered by this Treaty are promptly published or otherwise made publicly available.
   2. For purposes of this Article, "administrative ruling of general application" means an administrative ruling or interpretation that applies to all persons and fact situations that fall generally within its ambit and that establishes a norm of conduct but does not include:
   (a) a determination or ruling made in an administrative or quasi-judicial proceeding that applies to a particular covered investment or investor of the other Party in a specific case; or
   (b) a ruling that adjudicates with respect to a particular act or practice."

[9] Thus, for example, Article 15.2 of the BIT between Uruguay and the United States obliges the investor to provide information on its investment to the host Government in certain circumstances:
   "*Article 15: Special Formalities and Information Requirements*
   [...]
   2. Notwithstanding Articles 3 and 4, a Party may require an investor of the other Party, or its covered investment, to provide information concerning that investment solely for informational or statistical purposes. The Party shall protect any confidential business information from any disclosure that would prejudice the competitive position of the investor or the covered investment. Nothing in this paragraph shall be construed to prevent a Party from otherwise obtaining or disclosing information in connection with the equitable and good faith application of its law."

[10] See, for instance, the investment chapter of the Chile–United States FTA (2003).

[11] Although numerous ISDS tribunals tend to regard the two concepts as essentially synonymous, international legal doctrine has made a distinction between admissibility and jurisdiction. While "[...] *jurisdiction is the power of the tribunal to hear the case; admissibility is whether the case itself is defective – whether it is appropriate for the tribunal to hear it*". See *Waste Management, Inc. v. Mexico*, ICSID Case No. ARB(AF)/98/2, Dissenting Opinion of Keith Highet, 2 June 2000, para. 58. For a detailed discussion of the distinction between the two concepts, see Laird 2005.

[12] It could be said that the same applies to arbitration under ICSID.

[13] That is also the case of the FTAs between the United States and Singapore, and Peru, respectively.

[14] Furthermore, under the prevailing interpretation of "fork-in-the-road" provisions, as ISDS jurisprudence has shown, it is also easy to envisage situations in which an investor may submit a claim under ISDS procedures despite the existence of a "domestic forum" clause in an investment contract between the investor and the host country.

IV. IMPLICATIONS AND CONCLUSIONS

The significant increase in the number of ISDS disputes over the last decade represents in many ways a milestone in the evolution of international investment law. After being almost dormant in previous periods, ISDS activity during the last five years has generated a significant amount of cases touching on key procedural and substantive aspects, thus fostering the development of a jurisprudence that, although still in its early stages, will continue to evolve in the near future.

This section focuses on the implications that those developments have had on the countries involved. It analyses ISDS practice from different perspectives. First, what are the general features of the incipient jurisprudence emerging from ISDS practice? Second, what does that practice imply with respect to the operation of the system as a whole? Third, what are the implications of the two previous aspects for development? Fourth, as concluding remarks, an overall assessment will be made, including some observations regarding future IIA negotiations.

A. Legal perspective

As explained above (in chapter II), ISDS practice over the last decade has touched upon numerous procedural and substantive aspects of international arbitration and investment law. However, it should be noted that, despite the significant caseload, jurisprudence is still in its early stages, with the majority of cases submitted to arbitration during the last couple of years still pending. In that context, it is not surprising that most of the emerging patterns in jurisprudence relate to matters of jurisdiction and other procedural aspects, although some key substantive issues have also been addressed.

With respect to procedural matters, ISDS jurisprudence has focused on questions of jurisdiction and has clarified a number of issues that until recently had been discussed only theoretically. The jurisdictional objections have raised novel issues concerning, for example, the overlap of contractual and treaty-based disputes, the *jus standi* of minority and non-controlling shareholders, criteria to attribute to the host country measures adopted by State enterprises and the "fork-in-the-road" clauses. ISDS jurisprudence has addressed other key procedural issues in addition to jurisdictional questions, such as transparency and non-party participation in ISDS proceedings.

Regarding substantive aspects, ISDS jurisprudence, although less extensive, has dealt with key standards of treatment and protection of foreign investment. Salient issues addressed by ISDS jurisprudence during this initial period are the scope and content of the minimum standard of treatment and its related standards on fair and equitable treatment and full protection and security, the scope of the MFN principle, the methodology to determine whether there has been a breach of the national treatment standard and the criteria to determine whether an indirect expropriation has occurred.

It has been said of the evolving ISDS jurisprudence that consistency is one of its strengths. Frequently, however, there is evidence of almost identical disputes leading to conflicting results. Nonetheless, when ISDS experience is put into perspective, and bearing in mind that the jurisprudence is evolving on the basis of the interpretation of more than 2,500 different IIAs negotiated by different countries and containing provisions whose wording is also different, the degree of consistency in the evolving investment jurisprudence is quite remarkable.[1]

By contrast, conflicting decisions such as those in *Lauder* and *CME*[2] and the two SGS cases against Pakistan and Philippines have been relatively rare.

When one is inferring trends in ISDS jurisprudence, it is essential to act with extreme caution. It is quite difficult to extract the essence of the case law when the latter is based on the interpretation of texts of IIAs that, although they appear to be similar, in fact have provisions with different wording and thus entail very different legal effects. Furthermore, arbitral decisions are delivered on a given factual context, which is often unique to the dispute under consideration. Thus, it is not advisable to make general statements regarding the jurisprudential interpretation of a particular standard of treatment or protection. Any trend in this regard should always be placed in its appropriate context.

From a different perspective, however, it is possible to identify two important lessons derived from ISDS practice over the last decade. The first lesson is that the increase in investment disputes has tested the wisdom of negotiating IIAs with extremely broad and imprecise provisions. The broader and more imprecise a particular text is, the more likely that it will lead to different, and even conflicting, interpretations. This will increase not only the likelihood of a dispute arising between the investor and the host country, but also the possibility of delegating to the arbitral tribunal the task of identifying the meaning that the disputed provision should have. Clearly, one of the objectives of IIAs is to foster predictability and certainty for investors, but also for host countries, and in this regard, having investment provisions that are drafted broadly and imprecisely does not serve the interests of either of those parties.

The second lesson derived from ISDS practice is that, when negotiating IIAs, countries should not only pay attention to the particular wording of the agreement, but also bear in mind the future interaction between the IIA and the arbitration convention(s) referred to by the latter, particularly ICSID. As explained above (in section II), for a dispute to fall within the jurisdiction of ICSID, it is necessary to comply with the objective requirements of jurisdiction in Article 25 of the ICSID Convention. Thus, not everything that the parties agree shall be subject to arbitration under an IIA may in fact fall within the jurisdiction of ICSID.

B.   Systemic perspective

The procedural and substantive issues explained above have given rise to a number of concerns with regard to the proper functioning and overall legitimacy of ISDS. There is continuing debate about whether it is appropriate to use international arbitration as a means of dispute settlement that may rule on public policy issues without there being the same levels of safeguards for accountability and transparency that are typically required by domestic juridical systems. Furthermore, the growing number of investment disputes has increased Governments' and civil society's awareness of the potential consequences of entering into what might otherwise be seen as useful agreements. All these issues are important challenges that the international investment system, made up of a patchy network of a myriad of IIAs, is currently facing. It is therefore important to find out what Governments do in order to face those challenges. This paper shows that at least some countries have started to tackle the issues involved.

This study has focused on the major developments in international ISDS practice over the last decade and their influence on investment rulemaking. It has revealed a positive relationship between the last two variables. The development of a *new generation* of IIAs shows that several Governments have been attentive to the developments in ISDS practice. Observing how previous IIAs were interpreted and applied by arbitral tribunals, some Governments have come up with new provisions and new language, which address most of the problems that arose in the context of investment disputes. In this sense, it could be said that *new generation* IIAs represent those Governments' response to the various procedural and substantive issues raised in the context of ISDS practice over the period reviewed.

As explained in chapter III, in *new generation* IIAs the definition of "investment" has been made more precise, several provisions dealing with standards of protection have been redrafted and clarified, and the concept of transparency in the context of investment agreements has been improved and redefined. Furthermore, these IIAs have made it clear that investment protection and liberalization must not be pursued at the expense of other key public policy objectives, and have updated and modernized ISDS procedures, thus fostering an increase in information for civil society and increased participation by the latter in those procedures.

At the same time, most countries that are parties to the *new generation* IIAs are also still parties to numerous "old" IIAs containing provisions that use the same broad and imprecise language that has triggered investment disputes in previous years. The consequent risk of incoherence is especially high for developing countries that lack expertise and bargaining power in investment rulemaking and that may have to conduct negotiations on the basis of their negotiating partners' divergent model agreements. Already in the past, developing countries concluded different kinds of BITs, depending on whether their developed market economy treaty partner excluded pre-establishment obligations from the treaty or included them in it. With the recent emergence of more complex IIAs, an additional layer of potential incoherence has been introduced. At the same time it needs to be borne in mind that numerous "old" agreements are close to their initial date of expiration, a fact that enables countries to consider taking advantage of that juncture in order to modernize and update those agreements with the elements already incorporated in the *new generation* IIAs.

C.   Implications for development

As explained above, the increase in the number of investment disputes is associated with numerous challenges for developing countries. However, the existence of such challenges should not obscure the fact that the intensification of ISDS has two positive aspects for developing countries.

The first of these is the growing legal sophistication of investment dispute resolution. This serves the interests of all the parties involved – investors, developed countries and developing countries. However, since most developing countries lack the economic and political power of developed countries, they should be particularly interested in pursuing the further legalization of the international investment system. They benefit from further strengthening of the rule of law at the international level.

The second aspect is the possibility that increased ISDS may motivate host countries to improve domestic administrative practices and laws in order to avoid future disputes. Fostering greater rigour, discipline and due process in the application of legislation is a goal that should be pursued in every country, whether developing or developed. ISDS procedures could be instrumental in helping achieve that goal.

However, to make that happen, important capacity-building initiatives are necessary. In this regard, further work is recommended in a number of areas.

First, countries should improve their knowledge regarding how to use the international investment adjudication system. International investment law is a complex subject, with multiple sources and is in constant evolution. Thus, enhancing the domestic capacities of Governments and the private sector is paramount.

Furthermore, having more capable and informed government officials who fully understood the content and implications of IIAs, is not only in the interest of host countries but also in the best interest of foreign investors and home countries. Better-prepared officials are likely to increase the quality of domestic administration and domestic rulemaking and thereby reduce the need for foreign investors to invoke ISDS procedures to defend their interests. Moreover, if disputes cannot be avoided, the ability to participate directly in proceedings and defend the host countries against investors' claims would help ensure that the legitimacy of the ISDS system as a whole is improved.

Second, small and medium-sized enterprises (SMEs) – from developed and developing countries – should be able to participate in the ISDS system. Currently, the high cost of international arbitration proceedings, which amounts to several million dollars on average, limits access to international justice mainly to financially powerful investors. The majority of enterprises are SMEs which, if they became foreign investors, would start with relatively small operations and, most probably, in adjacent countries. Because of their limited size, lack of international experience and relative financial weakness, SMEs tend to be more vulnerable to arbitrary practices of host countries than TNCs.

Another potential initiative relates to one of the less acknowledged but significant benefits that IIAs can entail. IIAs are important not only because of their potential international impact in terms of attracting foreign direct investment or sending positive signals to foreign investors. Equally significant are promotion of transparency, due process and strict application of the rule of law, which are the best means of avoiding investment disputes. Through appropriate capacity-building, host countries could improve their administration of investment-related laws and regulations and, in this way, not only avoid being subject to investment disputes, but also improve the general investment climate.

A fourth area for action could be civil society. It is likely that the interaction between national investment policies and IIAs will trigger a broader political debate and foster awareness and provision of information about the importance and role of IIAs in general.

Furthermore, interaction between foreign investors and host countries is likely to continue to increase in the future.

Within this context, international organizations can play a role. As previously mentioned, capacity-building and international cooperation are required in order to allow Governments, foreign investors and civil society to fully understand and participate in further development of the international legal framework for foreign investment.

* * *

Notes

[1] Some legal scholars have recognized the degree of coherence in recent ISDS jurisprudence, and have drawn attention to the Argentine experience, in which the degree of consistency among different arbitration tribunals has been evident. For instance, it has been said that "[…] *l'exemple des onze décisions sur la compétence rendues dans les affaires argentines illustre parfaitement le mouvement de création d'une jurisprudence arbitrale beaucoup plus cohérente que son mode d'élaboration aurait pu le faire craindre.* " (Gaillard 2006).

[2] *CME Czech Republic B.V. v. Czech Republic*, UNCITRAL, Partial Award, 13 September 2001. Also *The Czech Republic v. CME Czech Republic B.V*, Court of Appeals, Stockholm, Sweden, Case No. T-8735-01 (42 ILM 919 (2003)).

REFERENCES

Coe, J. and N. Rubins (2005). "Regulatory expropriation and the Tecmed case: Context and contribution", in Weiler, T., ed., *International Investment Law and Arbitration: Leading Cases from the ICSID, NAFTA, Bilateral Treaties and Customary International Law* (London: Cameron May), pp. 597–668.

Gaillard, E. (2005). "Treaty-based jurisdiction: Broad dispute resolution clauses", *New York Law Journal*, Vol. 234, No. 68, pp. 1–3.

_____ (2006). "Chroniques des sentences arbitrales", *Centre international pour le règlement des différends relatifs aux investissements (CIRDI),* Revue trimestrielle, LexisNexis, Juris Classeur, January–February–March.

General Agreement on Tariffs and Trade (GATT) (1995). *Analytical Index: Guide to GATT Law and Practice* (Geneva: GATT), updated 6th edition.

Hamida, W. B. (2005). "The Mihaly v. Sri Lanka case: Some thoughts relating to the status of pre-investment expenditures", in Weiler, T., ed., *International Investment Law and Arbitration: Leading Cases from the ICSID, NAFTA, Bilateral Treaties and Customary International Law.* (London: Cameron May), pp. 47–76.

International Centre for Settlement of Investment Disputes (ICSID) Secretariat (2004). "Possible improvements of the framework for ICSID arbitration", Discussion Paper, available at (http://www.worldbank.org/icsid/highlights/improve-arb.pdf).

Laird, I. (2005). "A distinction without a difference? An examination of the concepts of admissibility and jurisdiction in Salini v. Jordan and Methanex v. USA", in Weiler, T., ed., *International Investment Law and Arbitration: Leading Cases from the ICSID, NAFTA, Bilateral Treaties and Customary International Law* (London: Cameron May), pp. 201–222.

Mendelson, M. (2005). "The runaway train: The 'Continuous Nationality Rule' from the Panevezys-Saldutiskis railway case to Loewen", in Weiler, T., ed., *International Investment Law and Arbitration: Leading Cases from ICSID, NAFTA, Bilateral Treaties and Customary International Law* (London: Cameron May), pp. 97–150.

Schreuer, C. (2001). *The ICSID Convention: A Commentary* (Cambridge: Cambridge University Press).

_____ (2005). "Investment treaty arbitration and jurisdiction over contract claims: The Vivendi I case considered", in Weiler, T., ed., *International Investment Law and Arbitration: Leading Cases from the ICSID, NAFTA, Bilateral Treaties and Customary International Law* (London: Cameron May), pp. 291–324.

United Nations Conference on Trade and Development (UNCTAD) (1998). *Bilateral Investment Treaties in the Mid-1990s* (New York and Geneva; United Nations), United Nations publication, Sales N. E.98.II.D.8.

_____ (1999a). *Admission and Establishment. UNCTAD Series on Issues in International Investment Agreements* (New York and Geneva: United Nations), United Nations publication, Sales No. E.99.II.D.10.

_____ (1999b). *National Treatment. UNCTAD Series on Issues in International Investment Agreements* (New York and Geneva: United Nations), United Nations publication, Sales No. E.99.II.D.16.

_____ (1999c). *Fair and Equitable Treatment. UNCTAD Series on Issues in International Investment Agreements* (New York and Geneva: United Nations), United Nations publication, Sales No. E.99.II.D.15.

_____ (1999d). *Most-Favoured-Nation Treatment. UNCTAD Series of Issues in International Investment Agreements* (New York and Geneva: United Nations), United Nations publication, Sales No. E.99.II.D.11.

_____(2000). *Taking of Property. UNCTAD Series on Issues in International Investment Agreements* (New York and Geneva: United Nations), United Nations publication, Sales No. E.00.II.D.4.

_____(2003). *Dispute Settlement: Investor–State. UNCTAD Series on Issues in International Investment Agreements* (New York and Geneva: United Nations), United Nations publication, Sales No. E.03.II.D.5.

_____ (2005a). *Investor–State Disputes Arising from Investment Treaties: A Review. UNCTAD Series on International Investment Policies for Development* (New York and Geneva: United Nations), United Nations publication, Sales No. E.06.II.D.1.

_____(2005b). *South–South Cooperation in International Investment Arrangements. UNCTAD Series on International Investment Policies for Development* (New York and Geneva: United Nations), United Nations publication, Sales No. E.05.II.D.26.

_____ (2005c). "Latest developments in investor–State dispute settlement", *IIA Monitor No. 4* (New York and Geneva: United Nations), United Nations publication, Document No UNCTAD/WEB/ITE/IIT/2005/2.

_____(2006a). *Investment Provisions in Economic Integration Agreements* (New York and Geneva: United Nations), United Nations publication, Document No. ITE/IIE/2005/10.

_____(2006b). *International Investment Arrangements: Trends and Emerging Issues. UNCTAD Series on International Investment Policies for Development* (New York and Geneva: United Nations) United Nations publication, Sales No. E.06.II.D.3.

_____(2006c). "Systemic issues in international investment agreements", *IIA Monitor No. 1* (New York and Geneva: United Nations), United Nations publication, Document No. UNCTAD/WEB/ITE/IIA/2006/2

_____(2006d). "Latest developments in investor–State dispute settlement", *IIA Monitor No. 4* (New York and Geneva: United Nations), United Nations publication, Document No NCTAD/WEB/ITE/IIT/2006/11.

_____ (2007). *Bilateral Investment Treaties 1995-2005: Trends in Investment Rulemaking* (New York and Geneva: United Nations), United Nations publication, Sales No. E.06.II.D.16.

ANNEX
List of cases reviewed

ADF Group Inc. v. United States of America, ICSID Case No. ARB(AF)/00/1, Final Award, 9 January 2003.

Aguas del Tunari S.A. v. Bolivia, ICSID Case No. ARB/02/3, Decision on Jurisdiction, 21 October 2005.

Alex Genin, Eastern Credit Limited v. Estonia, ICSID Case No. ARB/99/2, Award. 25 June 2001.

Amco Asia Corporation and others v. Indonesia, ICSID Case No. ARB/81/1, Decision on Jurisdiction, 25 September 1983 (1 ICSID Reports 394); Award, 20 November 1984.

American Manufacturing & Trading v. Zaire, ICSID Case No. ARB/93/1, Award, 21 February 1997 (reprinted in 12, *International Arbitration Reporter,* 1997, No. 4, pp. A-1 to A-2).

Antoine Goetz v. Republic of Burundi, ICSID Case No. ARB/95/3, Award, 10 February 1999.

Archer Daniels Midland Company & Tate & Lyle Ingredients Americas Inc. v. Mexico, ICSID Case No. ARB(AF)/04/5.

Asian Agricultural Products Ltd. v. Republic of Sri Lanka, ICSID Case No. ARB/87/3, Award, 27 June 1990.

Autopista Concesionada de Venezuela v. Venezuela, ICSID Case No. ARB/00/5, Decision on Jurisdiction, 27 September 2001.

Robert Azinian and others v. United Mexican States, ICSID Case No. ARB(AF)/97/2, 1 November 1999.

Azurix Corp. v. Argentina, ICSID Case No. ARB/01/12, Decision on Jurisdiction, 8 December 2003; Final Award, 14 July 2006.

Canfor Corp. v. United States of America, UNICITRAL, Notice of Arbitration, July 2002.

Case concerning East Timor, International Court of Justice, 1995 *ICJ Reports*, 89.

Case concerning the Barcelona Traction, Light and Power Company, Limited (Belgium v. Spain), 5 February 1970 (1970) International Court of Justice 3, at 35-36 (9 *International Legal Materials* 227).

Champion Trading v. Egypt, ICISD Case No. ARB/02/9, Decision on Jurisdiction, 21 October 2003.

CME Czech Republic B.V. v. Czech Republic, UNCITRAL, Partial Award, 13 September 2001. Also *The Czech Republic v. CME Czech Republic B.V*, Court of Appeal, Stockholm, Sweden, Case No. T-8735-01 (42 *International Legal Materials* 919 (2003)).

CMS Gas Transmission Company v. Argentine Republic, ICSID Case No. ARB/01/8, Decision on Jurisdiction, 17 July 2003; Award, 12 May 2005.

Compañía de Aguas del Aconquija & Vivendi Universal (formerly Compagnie Générale des Eaux) v. Argentina, ICSID Case No. ARB/97/3, Award, 21 November 2000; Annulment Tribunal: *Compañiá de Aguas del Aconquija & Vivendi Universal (formerly Compagnie Générale des Eaux) v. Argentine Republic*, ICSID Case No. ARB/97/3, Decision on Annulment, 3 July 2002.

Compañía de Desarrollo de Santa Elena S.A. v. Costa Rica, ICSID Case No. ARB/96/1, Award on the Merits, 17 February 2000.

Corn Products International, Inc. v. Mexico, ICSID Case No. ARB(AF)/04/1.

Emilio Agustin Maffezini v. The Kingdom of Spain, ICSID Case No. ARB/97/7, Decision on Jurisdiction, 25 January 2000; Award, 13 November 2000; Rectification of Award, 31 January 2001.

Enron and Ponderosa Assets v. Argentine Republic, ICSID Case No. ARB/01/3, Decision on Jurisdiction, 14 January 2004.

Eudoro Armando Olguín v. Republic of Paraguay, ICSID Case No. ARB/98/5, Award on Jurisdiction, 8 August 2000; Final Award 26 July 2001.

Eureko B.V. v. Poland, Ad-hoc arbitration procedure, Partial Award, 19 August 2005, available at (http://www.investmentclaims.com/ decisions/Eureko-Poland-LiabilityAward.pdf).

FEDAX N.V. v. Republic of Venezuela, ICSID Case No. ARB/96/3(1), Decision on Jurisdiction, 11 July 1997; Final Award, 9 March 1998.

GAMI Investments Inc. v. Mexico, UNCITRAL, Final Award, 15 November 2004.

Generation Ukraine, Inc. v. Ukraine, ICSID Case No. ARB/00/9, Award, 16 September 2003.

Holiday Inns S.A. and others v. Morocco, ICSID Case No. ARB/72/1, Decision on Jurisdiction, 12 May 1974.

Impregilo S.p.A v. Pakistan, ICSID Case No. ARB/02/2, Decision on Jurisdiction, 22 April 2005.

Iran-United States Claims Tribunal, Case N° A/18 of 6 April 1984 (5 Iran-U.S.C.T.R.-251).

Jack Rankin v. The Islamic Republic of Iran, Iran–United States Claims Tribunal, Award, 3 November 1987 (*Iran–United States Claims Tribunal Reports*, No. 17).

Joy Mining Machinery Limited v. Egypt, ICSID Case No. ARB/03/11, Decision on Jurisdiction, 6 August 2004.

Kaiser Bauxite v. Jamaica, ICSID Case No. ARB/74/3, Decision on Jurisdiction, 6 July 1975.

Klöckner Industrie-Anlagen GmbH and others v. Cameroon, ICSID Case No. ARB/81/2, Award, 21 October 1983 (2 ICSID Reports 16).

L.E.S.I-DIPENTA v. Algeria, ICSID Case No. ARB/03/8, Award, 10 January 2005.

Lanco International Inc. v. Argentina, ICSID Case No. ARB/97/6, Decision on Jurisdiction, 8 December 1998.

LG&E v. Argentina, ICSID Case No. ARB/02/1, Decision on Jurisdiction, 30 April 2004.

Liberian Eastern Timber Corporation (LETCO) v. Liberia, ICSID Case No. ARB/83/2, Decision on Jurisdiction, 24 October 1984 (2 *ICSID Reports* 349); Award, 31 March 1986.

Loewen Group, Inc. and Raymond Loewen v. United States of America, ICSID Case No. ARB(AF)/98/3, Award on Jurisdiction, 5 January 2001; Award on Merits, 26 June 2003.

Lucchetti S.A. and Lucchetti Peru S.A. v. Republic of Peru, ICSID Case No. ARB/03/4, Award, 7 February 2005.

Marvin Roy Feldman v. the United Mexican States, ICSID Case No. ARB(AF)/99/1, Award on the Merits, 16 December 2002.

Metalclad Corporation v. the United Mexican States, ICSID Case No. ARB(AF)/97/1, Award, 30 August 2000; Review by the British Columbia Supreme Court (2001 BCSC 664), 2 May 2001; Supplementary Reasons for BCSC Decision, 31 October 2001.

Methanex v. United States, UNCITRAL, Decision on *Amici Curiae*, 15 January 2001; Preliminary Award on Jurisdiction and Admissibility, 7 August 2002; Final Award, 3 August 2005.

Middle East Cement Shipping and Handling Co. S. A. v. Arab Republic of Egypt, ICSID Case No. ARB/99/6, Award, 12 April 2002.

Mihaly International Corporation v. Sri Lanka, ICSID Case No. ARB/00/2, Award, 15 March 2002.

Mondev International Ltd. v. United States of America, ICSID Case No. ARB(AF)/99/2, Award, 11 October 2002.

MTD Equity Sdn. Bhd. & MTD Chile S.A. v. Chile, ICSID Case No. ARB/01/7, Final Award, 25 May 2004.

Nottebohm Case (Liechtenstein v. Guatemala), International Court of Justice, 1955.

Occidental Exploration and Production Company v. Ecuador, London Court of International Arbitration, Case No. UN 346, Award, 1 July 2004.

Plama Consortium Limited v. Bulgaria, ICSID Case No. ARB/03/24, Decision on Jurisdiction, 8 February 2005.

Pope & Talbot, Inc. v. the Government of Canada, UNCITRAL, Interim Award on Merits, 26 June 2000; Award on the Merits, 10 April 2001; Award on Damages, 31 May 2002; Award on Costs, 26 November 2002.

PSEG Global, Inc., The North American Coal Corporation, and KonyaIngin Electrik Uretim ve Ticaret Limited Sirketi v. Turkey, ICSID Case No. ARB/02/5, Decision on Jurisdiction, 4 June 2004.

Ronald S. Lauder v. Czech Republic, UNCITRAL, Final Award, 3 September 2001.

S.A.R.L. Benvenuti & Bonfant v. Congo, ICISD Case No. ARB/77/2, Award, 8 August 1989.

S.D. Myers, Inc. v. Canada, UNCITRAL, First Partial Award, 13 November 2000.

Salini Costruttori S.p.A. and Italstrade S.p.A. v. Jordan, ICSID Case No. ARB/02/13, Decision on Jurisdiction, 9 November 2004.

Salini Construtorri S.p.A. and Italstrade S.p.A. v. Morocco, ICSID Case No. ARB/00/4, Decision on Jurisdiction, 23 July 2001.

SGS v. Pakistan, ICSID Case No. ARB/01/13, Decision on Jurisdiction, 6 August 2003.

SGS v. Philippines, ICSID Case No. ARB/02/6, Decision on Jurisdiction, 29 January 2004.

Siemens v. Argentina, ICSID Case No. ARB/02/8, Decision on Jurisdiction, 3 August 2004.

Société Ouest Africaine des Bétons Industriels (SOABI) v. Senegal, ICSID Case No. ARB/82/1, Decision on Jurisdiction, 1 August 1984.

Soufraki v. United Arab Emirates, ICSID Case No. ARB/02/7, Award, 7 July 2004.

Southern Pacific Properties v. Egypt, ICISD Case No. ARB/84/3, Decision on Jurisdiction, 27 November 1985.

Tecnicas Medioambientales Tecmed S.A. v. United Mexican States, ICSID Case No. ARB(AF)/00/2, Final Award, 29 May 2003.

Tembec Inc. v. United States of America, UNICITRAL, Notice of Arbitration, December 2003.

Terminal Forest Products Ltd. v. United States of America, UNICITRAL, Notice of Arbitration, March 2004.

Tokois Tokelés v. Ukraine, ICSID Case No. ARB/02/18, Decision on Jurisdiction, 29 April 2004; Dissenting Opinion, 29 April 2004.

United Parcel Service of America Ltd. v. the Government of Canada, UNICITRAL, Award on Jurisdiction, 22 November 2002.

Vacuum Salt Products Limited v. Ghana, ICSID Case No. ARB/92/1, Award, 16 February 1994 (reprinted in *ICSID Review*, 1994, vol. 9, 1, pp. 71–101/1994).

Waste Management, Inc. v. United Mexican States, ICSID Case No. ARB(AF)/00/3, Final Award, 30 April 2004.

Wena Hotel Ltd v. Arab Republic of Egypt, ICSID Case No. ARB/98/4, Decision on Jurisdiction, 29 June 1999; Award on Merits, 8 December 2000; Decision on Annulment, 5 February 2002.

William Nagel v. Czech Republic, Stockholm Chamber of Commerce (SCC) Case 049/2002.

Zhinvali Development Limited v. Georgia, ICSID Case No. ARB/00/1, unpublished.

SELECTED RECENT UNCTAD PUBLICATIONS ON TRANSNATIONAL CORPORATIONS AND FOREIGN DIRECT INVESTMENT
(For more information, please visit www.unctad.org/en/pub)

A. SERIAL PUBLICATIONS

World Investment Reports
(For more information visit www.unctad.org/wir)

World Investment Report 2007. Transnational Corporations, Extractive Industries and Development. Sales No. E.07.II.D.9. $75. http://www.unctad.org/ en/docs//wir2007_en.pdf.

World Investment Report 2007. Transnational Corporations, Extractive Industries and Development. An Overview. 50 p. http://www.unctad.org/ en/docs/wir2007overview_en.pdf.

World Investment Report 2006. FDI from Developing and Transition Economies: Implications for Development. Sales No. E.06.II.D.11. $75. http://www.unctad.org/ en/docs//wir2006_en.pdf.

World Investment Report 2006. FDI from Developing and Transition Economies: Implications for Development. An Overview. 50 p. http://www.unctad.org/ en/docs/wir2006overview_en.pdf.

World Investment Report 2005. Transnational Corporations and the Internationalization of R&D. Sales No. E.05.II.D.10. $75. http://www.unctad.org/ en/docs//wir2005_en.pdf.

World Investment Report 2005. Transnational Corporations and the Internationalization of R&D. An Overview. 50 p. http://www.unctad.org/ en/docs/wir2005overview_en.pdf.

World Investment Report 2004. The Shift Towards Services. Sales No. E.04.II.D.36. $75. http://www.unctad.org/en/docs//wir2004_en.pdf.

World Investment Report 2004. The Shift Towards Services. An Overview. 62 p. http://www.unctad.org/en/docs/wir2004overview_en.pdf.

World Investment Report 2003. FDI Policies for Development: National and International Perspectives. Sales No. E.03.II.D.8. $49. http://www.unctad.org/ en/docs//wir2003_en.pdf.

World Investment Report 2003. FDI Polices for Development: National and International Perspectives. An Overview. 66 p. http://www.unctad.org/ en/docs/wir2003overview_en.pdf.

World Investment Report 2002: Transnational Corporations and Export Competitiveness. 352 p. Sales No. E.02.II.D.4. $49. http://www.unctad.org/ en/docs//wir2002_en.pdf.

World Investment Report 2002: Transnational Corporations and Export Competitiveness. An Overview. 66 p. http://www.unctad.org/en/docs/ wir2002overview_en.pdf.

World Investment Report 2001: Promoting Linkages. 356 p. Sales No. E.01.II.D.12 $49. http://www.unctad.org/wir/contents/wir01content.en.htm.

World Investment Report 2001: Promoting Linkages. An Overview. 67 p. http://www.unctad.org/wir/contents/wir01content.en.htm.

Ten Years of World Investment Reports: The Challenges Ahead. Proceedings of an UNCTAD special event on future challenges in the area of FDI. UNCTAD/ITE/Misc.45. http://www.unctad.org/wir.

World Investment Report 2000: Cross-border Mergers and Acquisitions and Development. 368 p. Sales No. E.99.II.D.20. $49. http://www.unctad.org/wir/ contents/wir00content.en.htm.

World Investment Report 2000: Cross-border Mergers and Acquisitions and Development. An Overview. 75 p. http://www.unctad.org/wir/contents/ wir00content.en.htm.

World Investment Directories
(For more information visit http://r0.unctad.org/en/subsites/dite/fdistats_files/WID2.htm)

World Investment Directory 2004: Latin America and the Caribbean. Volume IX. 599 p. Sales No. E.03.II.D.12. $25.

World Investment Directory 2003: Central and Eastern Europe. Vol. VIII. 397 p. Sales No. E.03.II.D.24. $80.

Investment Policy Reviews
(For more information visit http://www.unctad.orgi/pr)

Investment Policy Review – Rwanda. 130 p..Sales No. E.06.II.D.15.$25

Investment Policy Review – Colombia 73 p..Sales No. E06.II.D.4 $25

Investment Policy Review – Kenya. 126 p. Sales No. E.05.II.D.21. $25.

Investment Policy Review – Benin. 147 p. Sales No. F.04.II.D.43. $25.

Investment Policy Review – Sri Lanka. 89 p. No. E.04.II.D.19 $25

Investment Policy Review – Algeria. 110 p. Sales No. F04.II.D.30. $25.

Investment Policy Review – Nepal. 89 p. Sales No. E.03.II.D.17. $20.

Investment Policy Review – Lesotho. 105 p. Sales No. E.03.II.D.18. $15/18.

Investment Policy Review – Ghana. 103 p. Sales No. E.02.II.D.20. $20.

Investment Policy Review – Tanzania. 109 p. Sales No. E.02.II.D.6 $20.

Investment Policy Review – Botswana. 107 p. Sales No. E.01.II.D.I. $22.

Investment Policy Review – Ecuador. 136 p. Sales No. E.01.II D.31. $25.

Investment and Innovation Policy Review – Ethiopia. 130 p. UNCTAD/ITE/ IPC/Misc.4.

Investment Policy Review – Mauritius. 92 p. Sales No. E.01.II.D.11. $22.

Investment Policy Review – Peru. 109 p. Sales No. E.00.II.D.7. $22.

Investment Policy Review – Egypt. 119 p. Sales No. E.99.II.D.20. $19.

Investment Policy Review – Uganda. 71 p. Sales No. E.99.II.D.24. $15.

Investment Policy Review – Uzbekistan.. 65 p. UNCTAD/ITE/IIP/Misc. 13.

International Investment Instruments
(Fore more information visit http://www.unctad.org/iia)

International Investment Instruments: A Compendium. Vol. XIV. Sales No. E.05.II.D.8. 326 p. $60.

International Investment Instruments: A Compendium. Vol. XIII. Sales No. E.05.II.D.7. 358 p. $60.

International Investment Instruments: A Compendium. Vol. XII. Sales No. E.04.II.D.10. 364 p. $60.

International Investment Instruments: A Compendium. Vol. XI. 345 p. Sales No. E.04.II.D.9. $60. http://www.unctad.org/en/docs// dite4volxi_en.pdf.

International Investment Instruments: A Compendium. Vol. X. 353 p. Sales No. E.02.II.D.21. $60. http://www.unctad.org/en/docs/psdited3v9.en.pdf.

International Investment Instruments: A Compendium. Vol. IX. 353 p. Sales No. E.02.II.D.16. $60. http://www.unctad.org/en/docs/psdited3v9.en.pdf.

International Investment Instruments: A Compendium. Vol. VIII. 335 p. Sales No. E.02.II.D.15. $60. http://www.unctad.org/en/docs/psdited3v8.en.pdf.

International Investment Instruments: A Compendium. Vol. VII. 339 p. Sales No. E.02.II.D.14. $60. http://www.unctad.org/en/docs/psdited3v7.en.pdf.

International Investment Instruments: A Compendium. Vol. VI. 568 p. Sales No. E.01.II.D.34. $60. http://www.unctad.org/en/docs/ps1dited2v6_p1.en.pdf (part one).

International Investment Instruments: A Compendium. Vol. V. 505 p. Sales No. E.00.II.D.14. $55.

International Investment Instruments: A Compendium. Vol. IV. 319 p. Sales No. E.00.II.D.13. $55.

UNCTAD Investment Guides
(For more information visit http://www.unctad.org/Templates/Page.asp?intItemID=2705&lang=14)

An Investment Guide to Rwanda: Opportunities and Conditions. 79 p. UNCTAD/ITE/IIA/2006/3

An Investment Guide to Mali: Opportunities and Conditions. 68 p. UNCTAD/ITE/IIA/2006/2.

An Investment Guide to Kenya: Opportunities and Conditions. 92 p. UNCTAD/ITE/IIA/2005/2.

An Investment Guide to Tanzania: Opportunities and Conditions. 82 p. UNCTAD/ITE/IIA/2005/3.

An Investment Guide to the East African Community: Opportunities and Conditions. 109 p. UNCTAD/ITE/IIA2005/4.

An Investment Guide to Mauritania: Opportunities and Conditions. 80 p. UNCTAD/ITE/IIA/2004/4.

Guide de l'investissement au Mali: Opportunités et Conditions. 76 p. UNCTAD/ITE/IIA/2004/1.

An Investment Guide to Cambodia: Opportunities and Conditions. 89 p. UNCTAD/ITE/IIA/2003/6. http://www.unctad.org/en/docs//iteiia20036_en.pdf.

An Investment Guide to Nepal: Opportunities and Conditions. 97 p. UNCTAD/ITE/IIA/2003/2. http://www.unctad.org/en/docs/iteiia20032_en.pdf.

An Investment Guide to Mozambique: Opportunities and Conditions. 109 p. UNCTAD/ITE/IIA/4. http://www.unctad.org/en/docs/poiteiiad4.en.pdf.

An Investment Guide to Uganda: Opportunities and Conditions. 89 p. UNCTAD/ITE/IIA/2004/3.

An Investment Guide to Bangladesh: Opportunities and Conditions. 66 p. UNCTAD/ITE/IIT/Misc.29. http://www.unctad.org/en/docs/poiteiitm29.en.pdf.

An Investment Guide to Ethiopia: Opportunities and Conditions. 90 p. UNCTAD/ITE/IIA/2004/2.

International Investment Policies for Development
(Fore more information visit http://www.unctad.org/iia)

Preserving Flexibility in IIAs: The Use of Reservations. 104 p. Sales no.: E.06.II.D.14. $15.

International Investment Arrangements: Trends and Emerging Issues. 110 p. Sales No. E.06.II.D.03. $15.

Investor-State Disputes Arising from Investment Treaties: A Review. 106 p. Sales No. E.06.II.D.1 $15

South-South Cooperation in Investment Arrangements. 108 p. Sales No. E.05.II.D.26 $15.
International Investment Agreements in Services. 119 p. Sales No. E.05.II.D.15. $15.

The REIO Exception in MFN Treatment Clauses. 92 p. Sales No. E.05.II.D.1. $15.

Issues in International Investment Agreements
(Fore more information visit http://www.unctad.org/iia)

International Investment Agreements: Key Issues, Volumes I, II and *III.* Sales no.: E.05.II.D.6. $65.

State Contracts. 84 p. Sales No. E.05.II.D.5. $15.

Competition. 112 p. E.04.II.D.44. $ 15.

Key Terms and Concepts in IIAs: a Glossary. 232 p. Sales No. E.04.II.D.31. $15.

Incentives. 108 p. Sales No. E.04.II.D.6. $15.

Transparency. 118 p. Sales No. E.04.II.D.7. $15.

Dispute Settlement: State-State. 101 p. Sales No. E.03.II.D.6. $15.

Dispute Settlement: Investor-State. 125 p. Sales No. E.03.II.D.5. $15.

Transfer of Technology. 138 p. Sales No. E.01.II.D.33. $18.

Illicit Payments. 108 p. Sales No. E.01.II.D.20. $13.

Home Country Measures. 96 p. Sales No.E.01.II.D.19. $12.

Host Country Operational Measures. 109 p. Sales No E.01.II.D.18. $15.

Social Responsibility. 91 p. Sales No. E.01.II.D.4. $15.

Environment. 105 p. Sales No. E.01.II.D.3. $15.

Transfer of Funds. 68 p. Sales No. E.00.II.D.27. $12.

Flexibility for Development. 185 p. Sales No. E.00.II.D.6. $15.

Employment. 69 p. Sales No. E.00.II.D.15. $12.

Taxation. 111 p. Sales No. E.00.II.D.5. $12.

Taking of Property. 83 p. Sales No. E.00.II.D.4. $12.

National Treatment.. 94 p. Sales No. E.99.II.D.16. $12.

Admission and Establishment.. 69 p. Sales No. E.99.II.D.10. $12.

Trends in International Investment Agreements: An Overview. 133 p. Sales No. E.99.II.D.23. $12.

Lessons from the MAI. 52 p. Sales No. E.99.II.D.26. $10.

Fair and Equitable Treatment.. 85 p. Sales No. E.99.II.D.15. $12.

Transfer Pricing.. 71 p. Sales No. E.99.II.D.8. $12.

Scope and Definition. 93 p. Sales No. E.99.II.D.9. $12.

Most-Favoured Nation Treatment.. 57 p. Sales No. E.99.II.D.11. $12.

Investment-Related Trade Measures. 57 p. Sales No. E.99.II.D.12. $12.

Foreign Direct Investment and Development.. 74 p. Sales No. E.98.II.D.15. $12.

B. ASIT ADVISORY STUDIES
(Formerly Current Studies, Series B)

No. 17. *The World of Investment Promotion at a Glance: A survey of investment promotion practices.* UNCTAD/ITE/IPC/3.

No. 16. *Tax Incentives and Foreign Direct Investment: A Global Survey*. 180 p. Sales No. E.01.II.D.5. $23. Summary available from http://www.unctad.org/ asit/resumé.htm.

C. INDIVIDUAL STUDIES

Bilateral Investment Treaties 1995—2006: Trends in Investment Rulemaking. 172 p. Sales No. E.06.II.D.16. $30.

Investment Provisions in Economic Integration Agreements. 174 p. UNCTAD/ITE/IIT/2005/10.

Globalization of R&D and Developing Countries.. 242 p. Sales No. E.06.II.D.2. $35.

Prospects for Foreign Direct Investment and the Strategies of Transnational Corporations, 2005-2008. 74 p. Sales No. E.05.II.D.32. $18.

World Economic Situation and Prospects 2005. 136 p. Sales No. E. 05.II.C.2. $15. (Joint publication with the United Nations Department of Economic and Social Affairs.)

Foreign Direct Investment and Performance Requirements: New Evidence from Selected Countries. 318 p. Sales No. E.03.II.D.32. $35.http://www.unctad.org/ en/docs//iteiia20037_en.pdf

FDI in Land-Locked Developing Countries at a Glance. 112 p. UNCTAD/ITE/IIA/2003/5.

FDI in Least Developed Countries at a Glance: 2002. 136 p. UNCTAD/ITE/IIA/6. http://www.unctad.org/en/docs// iteiia6_en.pdf.

The Tradability of Consulting Services. 189 p. UNCTAD/ITE/IPC/Misc.8. http://www.unctad.org/en/docs/ poiteipcm8.en.pdf.

Foreign Direct Investment in Africa: Performance and Potential. 89 p. UNCTAD/ITE/IIT/Misc.15. Free of charge. Also available from http://www.unctad.org/en/docs/poiteiitm15.pdf.

*TNC-SME Linkages for Development: Issues–Experiences–Best Practices. Proceedings of the Special Round Table on TNCs, SMEs and Development, UNCTAD X, 15 February 2000, Bangkok, Thailand.*113 p. UNCTAD/ITE/TEB1. Free of charge.

Measures of the Transnationalization of Economic Activity. 93 p. Sales No. E.01.II.D.2. $20.

The Competitiveness Challenge: Transnational Corporations and Industrial Restructuring in Developing Countries. 283p. Sales No. E.00.II.D.35. $42.

FDI Determinants and TNC Strategies: The Case of Brazil. 195 p. Sales No. E.00.II.D.2. $35. Summary available from http://www.unctad.org/en/pub/ psiteiitd14.en.htm.

Studies on FDI and Development

TNCs and the Removal of Textiles and Clothing Quotas. 78 p. Sales No. E.05.II.D.20.

Measuring Restrictions on FDI in Services and Transition Economies, 56 p. Sales No. 06.II.D.13.

D. JOURNALS

Transnational Corporations Journal (formerly *The CTC Reporter*). Published three times a year. Annual subscription price: $45; individual issues $20. http://www.unctad.org/en/subsites/dite/1_itncs/1_tncs.htm.

United Nations publications may be obtained from bookstores and distributors throughout the world. Please consult your bookstore or write:

For Africa, Asia and Europe to:

Sales Section
United Nations Office at Geneva
Palais des Nations
CH-1211 Geneva 10
Switzerland
Tel: (41-22) 917-1234
Fax: (41-22) 917-0123
E-mail: unpubli@unog.ch

For Asia and the Pacific, the Caribbean, Latin America and North America to:

Sales Section
Room DC2-0853
United Nations Secretariat
New York, NY 10017
United States
Tel: (1-212) 963-8302 or (800) 253-9646
Fax: (1-212) 963-3489
E-mail: publications@un.org

All prices are quoted in United States dollars.

For further information on the work of the Division on Investment, Technology and Enterprise Development, UNCTAD, please address inquiries to:

United Nations Conference on Trade and Development
Division on Investment, Technology and Enterprise Development
Palais des Nations, Room E-10054
CH-1211 Geneva 10, Switzerland
Telephone: (41-22) 907-5651
Telefax: (41-22) 907-0498
http://www.unctad.org

QUESTIONNAIRE

Investor-State Dispute Settlement and Impact on Investment Rulemaking

Sales No.

In order to improve the quality and relevance of the work of the UNCTAD Division on Investment, Technology and Enterprise Development, it would be useful to receive the views of readers on this publication. It would therefore be greatly appreciated if you could complete the following questionnaire and return it to:

Readership Survey
UNCTAD Division on Investment, Technology and Enterprise Development
United Nations Office in Geneva
Palais des Nations, Room E-9123
CH-1211 Geneva 10, Switzerland
Fax: 41-22-917-0194

1. Name and address of respondent (optional):

   _____

   _____

2. Which of the following best describes your area of work?

Government	☐	Public enterprise	☐
Private enterprise	☐	Academic or research Institution	☐
International organisation	☐	Media	☐
Not-for-profit organisation	☐	Other (specify) _____	

3. In which country do you work? _____

4. What is your assessment of the contents of this publication?

   | Excellent | ☐ | Adequate | ☐ |
   | Good | ☐ | Poor | ☐ |

5. How useful is this publication to your work?

   | Very useful | ☐ | Somewhat useful | ☐ | Irrelevant | ☐ |

6. Please indicate the three things you liked best about this publication:

   _____

   _____

   _____

7. Please indicate the three things you liked least about this publication:

   _____

   _____

   _____

8. If you have read other publications of the UNCTD Division on Investment, Enterprise Development and Technology, what is your overall assessment of them?

   | Consistently good | ☐ | Usually good, but with some exceptions | ☐ |
   | Generally mediocre | ☐ | Poor | ☐ |

9. On the average, how useful are those publications to you in your work?

Very useful   ☐   Somewhat useful   ☐   Irrelevant   ☐

10. Are you a regular recipient of Transnational Corporations (formerly The CTC Reporter), UNCTAD-DITE's tri-annual refereed journal?

Yes   ☐   No   ☐

If not, please check here if you would like to receive a sample copy sent to the name and address you have given above   ☐